Morning Meeting, Afternoon Wrap-Up

Morning Meeting, Afternoon Wrap-Up

Motivate Kids, Teach to Their Strengths, *and* Meet Your State's Standards

by Donna Whyte

Crystal Springs
BOOKS
A division of SDE Staff Development for Educators

Peterborough, New Hampshire

Published by Crystal Springs Books
A division of Staff Development for Educators
10 Sharon Road, PO Box 500
Peterborough, NH 03458
1-800-321-0401
www.crystalsprings.com
www.sde.com
© 2004 Crystal Springs Books
Published 2004
Printed in the United States of America

08 07   3 4 5

ISBN-10: 1-884548-65-2
ISBN-13: 978-1-884548-65-9

Library of Congress Cataloging-in-Publication Data

Whyte, Donna, 1962-
    Morning meeting, afternoon wrap-up : motivate kids, teach to their strengths, and meet your state's standards / by Donna Whyte.
        p. cm.
    Includes bibliographical references and index.
    ISBN 1-884548-65-2
    1. Classroom environment—United States. 2. Motivation in education—United States. 3. Effective teaching—United States. I. Title.
    LB3013.W49 2004
    370.15'4—dc22

                        2004013690

Editor: Sharon Smith
Art Director, Designer, and Production Coordinator: Soosen Dunholter
Illustrator: Joyce Orchard Garamella

Author's Note: The incidents that are used as examples in this book are real. The names of the children are not. I've changed the names, and occasionally combined separate incidents, to protect the privacy of the children in my classes.

This book is dedicated to the late Joseph Tourville, and to all the other teachers who may never truly know what they mean to their students.

CONTENTS

Introduction 9

Making Meetings Work for You 11

Have You Been Here? 11

The Goals 13

Creating a Strong Learning Environment 17

How Meetings Can *Save* You Time 17

That Magic Word: *Standards* 18

"You Don't Know the Trying Child I Have!" 19

Maslow's Hierarchy of Needs 22

Creating Problem-Solvers 24

Setting the Rules 25

The Student Teacher 26

What Does a Meeting Area Look Like? 28

Morning Meeting 33

Getting Started 33

Morning Message 40

You Gotta Have Movement! 65

The Schedule 67

The Calendar 73

Interactive Bulletin Boards 79

A Final Word About Morning Meeting 86

Afternoon Wrap-Up

Afternoon Wrap-Up 91

What's Different About Afternoon Wrap-Up 91

Back to the Home/School Folders 98

Changing the Pace 117

Games for Review & Assessment 123

Learning on the Way Out the Door 149

How I Believe Children Learn Best 152

What's Your Philosophy? 153

Resources

Resources 155

Bibliography 155

Index 156

ACKNOWLEDGMENTS

This book would not exist had it not been for the hard work and dedication of my editor, Sharon Smith. She was able to take my thoughts and translate them into a teaching tool for me to share. My sincere thanks to her.

Thanks also to Soosen Dunholter and Joyce Orchard Garamella, the book's designer and illustrator. Their imagination, hard work, and professional expertise have made the whole thing just the kind of serious fun that I wanted it to be.

INTRODUCTION

One of the important bases of good teaching is establishing a strong "learning environment" in your classroom. When I was teaching full-time, I was continually reminded of how important it is to create a classroom where children feel they belong. That's essential to the learning environment. Later, as I had an opportunity to visit many classrooms, I began to wonder what it is that creates classrooms where children care, are responsible, and love to learn.

I've taught and observed for years now, and what I've seen and experienced has convinced me: the classrooms that have those strong "learning environments"—the ones where kids feel they belong and are encouraged to succeed—are the ones where teachers teach more than facts. They teach life skills. These skills are so embedded in the curriculum that it's hard to imagine a successful curriculum without life skills. In these classrooms the teachers listen to the children. They share class discussions with the kids. They learn to differentiate instruction by responding to the many levels of participation.

These teachers put the focus where it belongs: on the kids.

I want to tell you about a way you can do that for your kids.

MAKING MEETINGS WORK FOR YOU

Have You Been Here?

Take a look at your classroom. Every teacher can relate to this. If you're a teacher, you'll see some piece of yourself in this. What happens when the kids come in in the morning? You're all hyper. You've had a lot to do. You've just run off the day's materials. You've gathered your supplies. You've barely gotten coffee. You've got to get going. They're already here at the door. So you're clapping your hands and you're saying, "Come on, guys, we've got to get going. Do you have your pencil? Where's your journal? Do you have your book? Come on, hon, get your coat off. You've got to put that coat away. Hon, get that lunch box. Come on, we've got to get a move on! We have a lot to do today!" These little kids are overwhelmed before they even start the day.

The other end of that is even worse. See whether you see your classroom in this. You've been doing a project today. Time has slipped away from you. The glue's on the table. The glitter's up your nose and on your arms. And you look up and say, "Oh, my gosh, the buses are here! Let's go! You guys aren't staying with me today! Everybody get packed up!" And you're running around like a chicken with its head cut off. And they're running next to you. You're yelling things like "Get your note!" "Where's your lunch box?" "Do you have the book you're supposed to take home?" And they go out the door. You finally get them to the bus. Nobody's spending the night. You go back to the classroom and you sit down and look around. Disaster. There's the note. There's the lunch box, the mitten, the coat. There was no wrap-up to the day. It was run 'em in, run 'em out, get 'em to the bus on time.

We've all lived there. But I wanted to change that for kids. It can't be good. It wouldn't be good for us—how can it be good for them? So I wanted to develop a routine for them that would let them start and end the day in a way that established and reinforced that strong environment for learning. And the way I did that was with Morning Meeting and Afternoon Wrap-Up.

The Goals

You may well be running meetings in your classroom already. Lots of teachers across the country are already holding a Morning Meeting, and some are doing an Afternoon Wrap-Up. What they do during them differs. And the other thing that differs is their goals.

You can make Morning Meeting and Afternoon Wrap-Up more effective for your kids if you know what your goals are. These are mine.

Building Community

C. Charles said in the results of his 2002 research that the majority of today's classroom management programs stress the importance of community building for success. This builds on the theory Abraham Maslow presented 50 years ago as part of his "Hierarchy of Needs": building a sense of community creates a "group effort" that encourages learning.

I'll get back to Maslow, because I think his work is incredibly important. But for now, let's just say that one of my goals is to create a group effort in my classroom. I'm not the only teacher. I learn by listening to the kids. They learn by listening to one another. And so we need to create that group effort. I want to encourage interaction among classmates.

Establishing a Routine

I want to develop a routine for the beginning and end of the day. We all need a routine that makes us feel good about the beginning and end of the day. We need a time at the beginning of the day when we learn what to expect that day. We need a time at the end of the day when we can reflect on what happened that day and prepare for the next day. Morning Meeting and Afternoon Wrap-Up develop routines for the beginning and end of the day.

This isn't just my theory. Wong and Wong write of the importance of remembering that "it is the procedures that set the class up for success to take place." Establishing routines that let children become members of a community helps create positive

Morning Meeting
"A Beginning to the Day"
Time for setting goals and getting started

Afternoon Wrap-Up
"An End to the Day"
Time for review, reflection, and looking forward

relationships—and those relationships help build effective learning environments.

Integrating the Five Components of Teaching Literacy

There are five components to teaching literacy: reading, writing, listening, speaking, and viewing. Children need daily practice in all of them. If I send a child to his seat to read a book, that's covering reading and, if there are pictures in the book, maybe viewing. If I send the child to a center to do an art project, he might be doing some listening because there are other children at the center. He's probably speaking, and he's viewing. But if you look at Morning Meeting and Afternoon Wrap-Up and the activities that go into those two times, these five elements are present every single day. Building those two segments into our day gives us as teachers an opportunity to introduce, practice, extend, and enrich what kids do every day in reading, writing, listening, speaking, and viewing.

Developing Higher-Level Thinking Skills

Many teachers know Bloom's Taxonomy, which talks about the levels of intellectual behavior that are important to learning. In 1956, B.S. Bloom identified presentation, exploration, analysis, prediction, synthesis, and application as keys to learning. In Morning Meeting and Afternoon Wrap-Up, children are called upon to share, listen for information, ask questions, predict what will happen, see situations from others' perspectives, and solve problems. That's pretty close to Bloom's. I'm absolutely convinced that students who develop all of these skills are bound to be wonderful learners.

Helping Kids Succeed

You may well be familiar with the work of William Glasser. His writings on "choice theory" discuss how important it is for our kids to have warm, supportive human relationships if they're going to succeed in school—and in the rest of their lives. Glasser said that an important part of building those relationships involves meeting four basic psychological needs: belonging, power, freedom, and fun. Morning Meeting and Afternoon Wrap-Up have to address those needs if they're going to help our kids become successful learners. Here's how they can do it:

Belonging. Morning Meeting and Afternoon Wrap-Up encourage a sense of community. They give kids regular opportunities to interact socially and to work as part of a group to solve problems together. We sing, dance, and laugh together. We share things about our lives. We get to know one another.

Power. In choice theory, power is defined as personal growth that enables the learner to acquire knowledge and skills and to attain goals and a feeling of self-worth. Morning Meeting and Afternoon Wrap-Up offer children that kind of power and self-esteem and give them a needed "voice" in their classroom.

Freedom. Morning Meeting and Afternoon Wrap-Up address the need for freedom from monotony by balancing routine with novelty. Meetings include discussions, a variety of instructional strategies, movement, and many different kinds of team-building activities.

Fun. Meetings revolve around games, songs, cooperation, and "learning to learn." They're designed to create excited and enthusiastic learners.

The Way We Choose to Start and End Our Day

- Speaks volumes about what we value in our classrooms
- Sets the stage for the day and the year
- Integrates reading, writing, listening, speaking, and viewing skills
- Emphasizes shared responsibility
- Builds problem solvers
- Offers safety
- Develops a climate of trust
- "Cements" our community

Providing Time for Assessment and Reflection

Meetings provide opportunities for daily assessment of children. And that means you can adapt your teaching based on what you find out. You can make your plan book reflect the needs of the class. If you say, "I don't have time to assess what they do in my reading group every day," then bring a piece of that into Morning Message and you can make an informal observation during that time. You can see then whether they're getting it. You can see whether they're keeping up with your reading series or whether they're meeting your school's standards for writing.

I always say to teachers, "It's so important for you to reflect on what's happening. Did they get it? How are you going to know if you never ask them?" I remember one time when we invited a man to come into our class every day for a week to teach children how to use tools safely. He talked about hammers and screwdrivers and goggles. His follow-up lesson was to build birdhouses with the class. So at the end of that week, when we got to Afternoon Wrap-Up, I asked the kids about what Mr. Jensen was doing. And little Amber said, "Who's Mr. Jensen?"

I admit I was taken aback by that! So I said, "Gee, Amber, who do you think that man is who's been visiting our classroom every day for a week? And what do you think he's been doing here?" You know what she said? She said that she didn't know who he was, but she thought he was walking around while I was teaching kids to make birdhouses.

Sometimes it can be really enlightening to find out how children see the world. I think Amber assumed that I was the only person in our class who taught. She never connected a new adult with that role.

What concerns me is that if there is never an opportunity to let children express what they think and what they've learned, we may never really know what's in their heads. Afternoon Wrap-Up gives Amber the chance to say what she thinks. And it gives me the chance to adapt my teaching to what she needs.

We all say that we don't have time. But Afternoon Wrap-Up gives you a quick little insight into what really happened today. Did they get the big picture? "We had fun." That's not good enough. Did we meet the essential questions of what we were trying to do today in the lessons that we did? That's important.

Creating a Strong Learning Environment

It's my hope that you and your students will benefit educationally from the suggestions for Morning Meeting and Afternoon Wrap-Up that are provided in the following pages. And I also hope that the ideas here will help you and your students work, learn, and have fun in a more rewarding environment.

Always remember that the class that begins and ends together . . . learns together!

How Meetings Can *Save* You Time

Across the United States, people are constantly telling me, "I don't have enough time." I agree. We *don't* have enough time. But sometimes we're not utilizing our time in the best way.

People think Morning Meeting and Afternoon Wrap-Up take too long and take too much time from teaching. I believe it's time we can't afford *not* to spend. I wanted to create a Morning Meeting and Afternoon Wrap-Up that made my day longer by giving me more teaching time. I wanted a time when I could sit up front and introduce a whole-group lesson to kids or maybe show them a new center I was going to set up. They were able to ask questions about it, and I could see the leveling.

Some of the kids were going, "Um-hmm. Already know." And I'd say, "Okay. You're off." I'd send them right off to independent work time. With others, it might be: "You don't understand? You stay." Some kids might have had a quick question for me, or they might have been able to figure out the answer by asking a friend. So Morning Meeting was a time at the beginning of our day when I could start to see where the kids were and to assess them at that level.

Morning Meeting and Afternoon Wrap-Up were also the times when we were going to build community. In our battle for time, Ruth Charney wrote, "we need to remember that academics and social behavior are profoundly intertwined." Building better learners requires building community. And building community means building social skills—life skills.

That Magic Word: *Standards*

I used to keep a calendar behind my desk that showed things that I wanted to touch on each month. And I'd look back and say, "Hmm. Teaching them how to sequence a story. I didn't do that in September. I'd better figure out how to get to that in October." I usually could find a way to take just about any standard and somehow work it into Morning Meeting and Afternoon Wrap-Up.

You can see for yourself whether it works. Just take a piece of paper and list some of your own state standards. Then start checking things off.

In Morning Meeting and Afternoon Wrap-Up, for example, we read to children. We let children read by themselves. We read *with* children. If one of my state standards says that children will learn to connect pictures in books with the print, then I'll incorporate that into Morning Meeting. I'll say, "Here's a bike in the picture. Can anybody find the word *bike* down here in the print?" Does what you're teaching in Morning Meeting and Afternoon Wrap-Up help your kids meet the standards? If it does, check it off. Look at each of your standards and ask, "Did we address that in either Morning Meeting or Afternoon Wrap-Up?" If you did, check it off and mark the date. And then review that as often as you feel is necessary. You can see for yourself whether Morning Meeting and Afternoon Wrap-Up are helping you meet the standards.

"You Don't Know the Trying Child I Have!"

Sometimes teachers say to me, "Your ideas sound great, but you don't know the trying child I have." And I think, "I *was* the trying child you have!"

I remember talking to a group of teachers one time and saying, "What will happen to these kids? They talk back. They spit. They bite. They run. They don't do anything you tell them to. What will happen to them?" And one of the teachers said, "They'll end up in jail." Or maybe they'll end up speaking to you some day. Because that was me.

I often share that I was a very difficult student. I didn't follow directions. I had many behavior issues. I was often out of control. There are kids with behavior issues who have nothing wrong with them academically. I was smart. I wasn't social smart. I was a nightmare of a child.

But Mr. Tourville changed my life. He single-handedly changed my life when I was 11 years old. Did he change my behavior? No. But he was the first teacher I ever met who knew exactly how to handle me.

I walked into Mr. Tourville's classroom with an attitude. I said to him, "I bet you weren't happy to see *me* on your list!" And he said, "Oh, Miss Black [my name then], I was very happy to see your name on my list because I'm always up for a good challenge." He had a big smile all over his face. I remember thinking, "Does this guy *want* me in his class?" I went back and sat down and thought, "What's *his* gig?"

He said I was putty in his hands after that. And I say it all goes back to the fact that I thought, "Finally, maybe this is where I belong. Because he doesn't mind having me." Everybody else already knew what I was. My mother always used to say that if there had been speed dial on the principal's phone then, our number would have been at the top.

Mr. Tourville knew all that, and he made me feel like a part of his classroom anyway.

Mr. Tourville was life-altering.

He never made the mistake other people made, which was believing that they could control me. They wanted to control me by threatening me and bribing me. Those are the two ways in which we try to control kids in our school system.

I'll threaten you: "I'll call your mother!" And you think, "Go ahead and call my mother. She doesn't answer the phone for bill collectors; she's not going to answer it for you!" So I don't care if you call my mother. That's not a threat that's going to mean anything to me.

The other thing teachers do to try to control kids is bribe them: "I'll give you a sticker if you stay in your seat." If I'm a kid, I can probably do that. But I'll stay in my seat only till I get what I want. Then I'll go back to being me. The bribe doesn't change my behavior long term. Believe me, I know what it feels like to be the teacher who's trying to change this behavior. I've been there. It feels as though there's no other choice. And if the goal is to get that student to do something immediately, you do what you have to do. But recognize that if your goal is to change behavior over the long term, bribery won't work.

Mr. Tourville didn't try to control me. He gave me a gift. He taught me to control myself. When I made bad choices, he would say, "That was not a very smart choice, Miss Black. You need to live with the consequence of that, and the consequence is that now you're not going to be part of the group." And he was always very matter-of-fact. He didn't sound mad. He wasn't mad at me. He wasn't screaming at me. He didn't look mad. He just matter-of-factly stated, "It was your choice, hon."

Mr. Tourville was the model I wanted to emulate when I started teaching kids. And at the beginning of the first year I taught, I didn't.

(continued on page 22)

The Importance of Nonverbal Signals

When you're trying to run a meeting, you don't want to be saying, "Chelsea, hon, get your finger out of your nose." Or "Nathan, stop punching the person next to you." So it helps to have nonverbal signals that the kids recognize. And then they also need to understand that there's a consequence to not reacting to that signal. Nonverbal signals can get the kids back on track.

Even if you're not the speaker, it's great when things are going well in Morning Meeting to let the kids know. If the student teacher is doing the interactive chart and you see that the kids are paying attention, hold up the smiley face attached to a craft stick. And if things aren't going well, flip the stick over so that they see that face with a frown. You don't have to say a word. All you have to do is turn the stick.

I used to take these faces to assemblies. My principal used to make fun of me. He said, "I see that grouch face come out and everybody starts sinking in his chair." It's a visual clue that what you're doing is not okay. Good choice (showing smiley face). Bad choice (showing grouchy face). If I'm staring at you and I tap the grouch face three times, you need to either make a different choice or leave the group. I may need to stop the group and move you, but I'm going to give you a couple of seconds to make a different choice. It gives the kids a warning. It also avoids having one interruption after another.

You can use the reproducibles on page 44. Or if you'd rather, you can make something similar out of those little foam hands (thumbs-up, thumbs-down) you buy at a craft store. Use them to indicate good choice and bad choice. So often I would say, "Was that a good choice?" And after a while the kids would start giving a thumbs-up. Eventually all I had to do was stand on the other side of the room and show the signal.

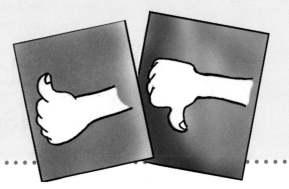

I was all the worst teachers I'd ever had. I screamed all the time. I thought, "This is crazy. I don't want to be a teacher. This is awful." That lasted about two weeks. Then I realized, it's awful because I'm thinking I can control this classroom, that it's mine, and that I need to take control. And it's not mine. I decided that I don't want to control children. I want to teach children to control themselves.

And that was the key.

When you start thinking about teaching kids to control themselves, it makes you look at things differently. Maybe Andy is a kid in your classroom, and Andy doesn't sit still. You know what? *I* don't sit still. Is that a terrible life thing? I've been lucky enough to get some great comments when teachers evaluate my presentations. But what's amazing to me is how many of those comments are positive spins on things that were considered so negative when I was a kid.

Take a comment like "She's so outgoing!" That used to be "She's never quiet!"

Now they say, "I love your energy!" Then they said, "She has too much energy! She doesn't sit still and stay in her seat. Her feet move all the time."

It's right on my report card. I brought out my report cards, and one of them said, "She never uses the materials appropriately." You know what people say now? "Wow! You have so many creative ideas!"

So when you work with those trying kids in your class, work on ways to find the good things in those kids now. Don't wait till they're grown up.

Maslow's Hierarchy of Needs

I'm a big believer in Maslow's Hierarchy of Needs. Maslow's Hierarchy is basically a pyramid. Way down at the bottom of the pyramid are the physiological needs. There are kids who aren't fed, who aren't sleeping, who don't have shelter. When kids are focusing all their attention on those basic human needs, it's very hard to get them to move up the pyramid to the point where they're learning.

The second level of the pyramid is physical and emotional safety. If a child doesn't feel safe in the classroom, he's not going to be able to move up the hierarchy. Learning is way up at the top.

On the pyramid, the next level after physical and safety needs is the need for a sense of community/belonging. I'm wondering how, in classrooms across the country, those needs for community are being met. We need to create communities in our schools where we believe that kids can become learners. So I want to build a sense of community. And building that means that the kids come together and they feel it's their classroom. Kids need to feel "part of something."

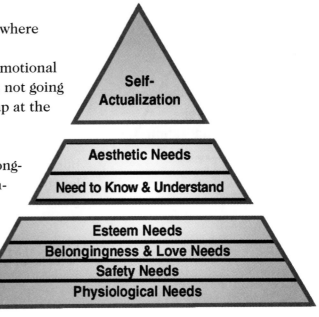

Maslow's Hierarchy in Action

One year when I was working as a teacher in a second-grade classroom, I remember, bomb threats started coming in to the principal's office. A high school student was calling them in. Every day we were closing down classrooms, and this voice would come over the loudspeaker.

The code was "Dr. Marcus is in the building." And that meant you closed the doors, closed the blinds, got the kids away from the windows, and stayed in the classroom. You didn't go to specials, you didn't go to lunch, nothing. So you'd better have some crackers in the classroom. This went on for four days in a row—bomb scares every day. And the fourth day, this little guy—I can still see him—said, "Oh, I hate it when that Dr. Marcus comes! We never get to go to lunch!" I can still see his little face: "He's in the building again!"

That afternoon a teacher in the faculty room said, "I don't mind it so much. They're really getting a lot done." And I remember whipping around and saying, "You are so fooling yourself." Those kids were stuck down at the safety-needs level of the pyramid. There was an emotional and physical safety-needs issue. I don't care whether the little ones seemed to not notice. I would have dared to walk into any classroom in that school and ask the kids what they'd done that past week, and they would have come back every single time to what was going on related to safety. That's the way it works. So it really is upsetting to me to know that some teachers believe that kids can focus on learning when there are other issues involved.

Self-Actualization

Way up at the top of the pyramid is what Maslow calls "self-actualization." I call it "learning." It's where you can become a thinker and a doer. If you're concentrating all your efforts at the lower levels, you never get to that top part. You need a base. So you can't have good teaching without doing things every day that set up this base. That's where it always starts for me.

If a kid comes in the door in the morning and his first question is "What's for snack?" and his second question is "What's for lunch?"—forget whatever you thought you were doing with this child. He's hungry!

Creating Problem-Solvers

If we're going to address Maslow's Hierarchy, we have to pay attention to the need for community. We have to be sure that physical needs are met and that emotional and physical safety needs are met, but then I think it's really important to build a community in the classroom. We want to create an environment in which learning is a group effort. We need to encourage interaction among students.

One way to do that is to train kids to answer some of their own questions—but they can't do that if they don't have speech and listening skills. I want to train every teacher to stick a rubber ball in her pocket. When a child asks you a question or makes a statement that suggests she's asking you to solve a problem, think of yourself as that rubber ball and just bounce it back.

"I don't have a pencil."

"What do you do if you don't have a pencil?"

"Have you seen my journal?"

"I don't have your journal, sweetie. Why don't you go look where you think you might have left it?"

"She said that . . . Amy said that . . . Cody said that Ben doesn't like me."

"Let's see. I don't hear my name in there, so I must not be involved, sweetie. What are you going to do?"

The reality is that we need to stop solving their problems. We're spending much too much time in charge of everyone. I want to quit answering their questions and instead encourage them to talk to each other to solve problems. Getting them to do that takes training. Morning Meeting and Afternoon Wrap-Up can be the times when you constantly encourage them and model for them so that the kids get to see what it's like to have to talk to each other.

William Glasser and his choice theory had a huge effect on how I look at things—how I question kids, talk to kids, interpret what they say. Glasser talks about empowering children. How do we give kids power? You'll have fewer management problems if you give children in classrooms power. You do that by believing that they're part of the makeup of the class. It's not always me giving the lesson. You, the student, give the lesson. You have some power.

I think when you say "power," that's a scary thing to teachers. When you say, "You need to give the kids some power," teachers say, "Well, I'm not going to let them take over my class!" But remember the definition of power in choice theory? It's the kind of personal growth that lets the learner gain knowledge and skills, reach goals, and gain a feeling of self-worth. To achieve these goals, children need some say in their classrooms. It's not taking over. It's the kind of power that feels like "I'm the learner." And choice is built into that. It doesn't have to mean that the kids take over the classroom. It can be as simple as "Gee, I wonder what would help most. Would it help if we brought out the dice? Or would it help if we just wrote it on a piece of paper? What do you want to do?" It's empowering kids.

Setting the Rules

You need to set up your own rules for Morning Meeting and Afternoon Wrap-Up. I would never say I know what's best for your classroom; I'm not *in* your classroom. I don't know what's best in my own classroom from year to year until I meet the little guys and then find out what's best for them. But at the beginning of the year you do need to establish some classroom rules. And once you've set them, they need to be black and white. There can't be gray areas. I think gray areas drive kids to test the limits. I try to make sure that the rules are clear, that everyone knows what they are, and that when they don't follow them, there's a consequence.

The key to classroom management is to teach the student to control himself. "That wasn't a good choice. It's too bad, but that was the choice you made, and these are the consequences." Say it in a matter-of-fact way.

Carrie was a biter in my class. Kids don't want to sit next to biters. Suppose I say to you, "Hi. Can I sit here next to you? I bite." You'd say, "No way!" So there's a natural consequence to being a biter: nobody wants to sit next to you. So I told Carrie, "You sit over there." I wasn't the punisher; I wasn't the bad guy. "I'm sorry you're not a part of our group right now, but you're not following the group's rules. The group doesn't want to be bitten. So you sit over there, and when you change your mind and make a different choice, you may come back and join us again."

The Student Teacher

I'm tired of all those little jobs. It's easy to spend your whole Morning Meeting assigning jobs. We don't have time. If you want to get rid of those little jobs, I have an easy solution.

I used to wish I had a student teacher in my class. Then I finally realized, "You know what? I have a student teacher. From this day forward, I'll never have to apply for one." The mistake I made was not using all the student teachers I already had.

I said that one day to Tina, my coteacher, and the next day she said, "What are you going to do?"

I said, "I'm going to get rid of all those little jobs: Line up. Turn out the lights. Fill the mailboxes. They take too much time. I don't have time in class to be wasting. So . . . when the kids come in today, I'm going to ask them if they want to be the student teacher."

She said, "What are you going to do with them?"

I said, "Each day one child will be the student teacher. We'll just move down the list of kids. If you're a kid in this class and you're not here, we'll put the blue clothespin on your name on the list so we can come back to you. The student teacher will be in charge of all the jobs. That kid will help with Morning Message. He'll load the mailboxes. He'll do all the little jobs for the day."

Tina said, "I don't think they're going to like it. Kids like those little jobs you give them."

I said, "Okay, we'll see." My experience is that kids will like whatever you inspire them to like.

The next day I sat the kids down in Morning Meeting and I said, "You know what? You guys are my student teachers. Who wants to take down all those little jobs? We'll just rip the list right off the wall!" There's motivation right there! "And then, when you're the student teacher, you get to sit at the student teacher's desk. You get to wear the visor that says 'Student Teacher' on it. You get to do the messages. You're in charge of everything! It'll be like being teacher for the day every 22 days. You don't get to do it every day. You have to take turns with everybody in the class. But when it's your turn, you do all the jobs. So if you have that little crummy job like 'turn off

Student Teacher of the day

1	Matthew Brown	13	Melissa Smith
2	Eric Jones	14	Pedro Martinez
3	Kim Chang	15	Ben G___
4	Samantha F___	16	Jenny R___
5	Merissa R___	17	Evan R___
6	Sarah M___	18	Kristen R___
7	___	19	Sharon ___
8	___	20	Sonic ___
9	Anthony R___	21	B___
10	___	22	___ R___
11	Ya___ R___	23	Anna M___
12	Ca___	24	___

lights,' what if Mrs. Whyte doesn't need her lights turned off today? I say, you can have *all* the jobs. And then there'll be no little crummy jobs to do. There'll be just one big job for the day.

"But I don't want to decide for you. I think you guys should decide. If you're as excited as I am about having the desk and wearing the visor and everything, come over here and stand by the student teacher's desk." And then I said, "If you want to keep all those little jobs, the way Mrs. Davis likes, go and stand near Mrs. Davis."

They were all on my side of the room!

Tina said, "You tricked them!" But basically, having a "student teacher" eliminated that whole headache. (Yeah, yeah: It's the same thing as a teacher's helper, but they like it when I call it the student teacher.)

It's too easy to live every day letting those jobs eat up valuable time. You don't have time? Well, maybe that's because you just spent 15 minutes deciding who's going to take the messages.

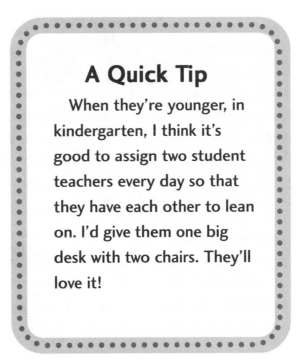

A Quick Tip

When they're younger, in kindergarten, I think it's good to assign two student teachers every day so that they have each other to lean on. I'd give them one big desk with two chairs. They'll love it!

What Does a Meeting Area Look Like?

I think the most important thing about a classroom meeting area is that the set-up should always let kids see one another's faces. At a dining table, would it be okay to talk with your back turned to the table? It's not okay in class either. Tina and I were forced out of the box. We'd never really thought about the way kids sat until we had Jonna and Emmie, two little hearing-impaired girls, in our class. And we realized, "Oh, my gosh! If they're behind this child and this child says something, that's not good! They're beginning to read lips, and we need to make sure

Sharing the Chair

Often I used to let the student teacher sit up front in a chair next to me or even take my chair. It started as a joke: I'd give away my chair if somebody could read the message. And the kids read it and I had to give away my chair and sit on the floor. They liked the chair.

Then I thought, "This chair could be multifaceted. I need to figure out a way to make it more versatile." That Morning Meeting chair could represent all kinds of things for our classroom. All I had to do was put Velcro on the chair and on a bunch of signs that I'd laminated. It's even easier for you. You can use the reproducibles on page 31. You laminate them, you put Velcro on the back of each one, and you rotate them.

So today it's the birthday chair. Tomorrow we don't have any birthdays, so we'll just make it the student teacher chair. If there's a special visitor, well, the student teacher's going to have to sit on the floor because we have a special visitor today. Get a separate chair—that's another one in addition to your chair—so that the kids feel that they do share a chair. Also, sometimes during Afternoon Wrap-Up, we'd play "Who Wants to Be the Teacher?" Everybody likes to sit in the chair when he's the teacher.

Sample Rules

As an example, here are some of the rules that the kids and I came up with. Maybe they'll give you something to play off when you think about what rules you might want to post in your meeting area.

Attention!
Eyes are on the speaker.
Ears are listening.
Hands and feet are still.
Voice is off.

Rules for Meeting Area

Raise your hand to speak.
Wait for the speaker to finish.
One person talks at a time.
"Look" like a good listener.
Participate.
Remember: people can disagree!
Your tone is as important as your words.

that everyone can see everyone else. We need to make sure that Jonna and Emmie can see not only this child's lips but also the expression on her face."

That was very hard in our classroom. We had to move a lot of furniture to get our kids in a circle, but it turned out to be a really good thing for everybody, not just Jonna and Emmie. It's good for all visual learners, and many children are visual learners. So I think your goal should always be to have kids facing kids. You want them to look one another in the eye and speak to one another. And when you're reading books or sharing an interactive chart, if you put the kids in rows, how are you going to determine the rotation of those rows? Is Amanda going to beat everybody to Morning Meeting every day and get the front spot? That's what she'll do if that's what you let her do. That's Amanda's personality.

If you absolutely can't manage a circle in your classroom, you need to have a set-up that rotates the rows. You need to say that these are the people in row 1 today. Where is row 1 going tomorrow? They're going to row 2. Where is row 2 going the next day? They're going to row 3. That way, eventually everyone gets a chance up front.

One of the things experts say about reading with kids is that the experience of reading at home should be re-created in the classroom, so that a kid feels as though that book is right in front of him. That's not going to happen if you let Amanda take the front place every time. You have to create that rotation, to get all the kids closer to you at some point. So if you're a teacher and you say, "I just can't do the circle," my second option would be that you have a way to rotate so that everybody gets a chance to be closer to the message.

So how the kids sit is the most important part of how the meeting space is set up. After that, here's how we did it: The interactive chart was the center of the activities. For us, chairs for me and for the student teacher or special person were next to the chart. Right behind me was the schedule. Right nearby was the calendar. And we had a cart that held all the tools. The pointers were sticking out, and the highlighting tape was right there.

If you want things to run smoothly, the tools need to be there. The kids liked that, because if I made a mistake, one of them would reach over and get the whiteout tape. It was great!

You need to set up your classroom meeting space to make it easy for kids to interact and learn together. And then you get to the fun part: what you do in that space. . . .

MORNING MEETING
GETTING STARTED

Think about how you typically begin the day with the kids in your classroom. Do you greet the kids at the door as they come in? If you do, good for you! I think it's important to greet kids at the door in the morning. It lets them know that you were expecting them and you're eager to see them. Treat them as if they were guests in your home. Would you ever say, "Hey, I'm in the closet getting the thing. I'll be right out!" Maybe once in a blue moon. But certainly you wouldn't do that on an ongoing basis. So I want to be there at the door. I want to greet the kids. And I want to establish a routine.

The Home/School Folder

For me, an important part of the morning routine is the home/school folder. That's the first thing the kids bring in in the morning and the last thing that goes out at night. At the beginning of the year, everybody gets a home/school folder to bring back and forth. It's just a standard school folder, but it's going to connect our classroom with the student's home. Anything the child's parents want me to see should be in there. Anything I want them to see will be in there. Every kid has one.

There's a letter I send home at the beginning of the year about the home/school folder. It tells the parents, "This is your connection to me. This is my connection to you." The letter looks something like the reproducible on page 35. If you want, you can just make copies of that letter and sign your name at the bottom.

I like to use a folder with two pockets; it helps teach the concept of left and right. The left side is for "Left at Home," so if something is in here, you (the student) leave it at home. The right side is "Bring Right Back," meaning you need to bring these papers back with you when you come to class. If you take a paper out of the right side and do your homework, you need to put it back in so that it comes back to school. But if you're taking home

What Can You Tell from a Face?

When the kids come in in the morning, you need to pay attention to their faces. A face can tell you a lot about what kind of day that kid is having. I could take one look at Jason's face and realize he was having problems. Maybe he'd gotten in trouble on the bus that morning. Then he'd lost his coat in the bus room. The cafeteria had had his favorite, French toast sticks, at breakfast, but they had run out before he'd gotten there. So this kid was already a wreck when he got to class.

You have to be sure to recognize that. You have to ask what happened and then say something like, "Jase, you've gotten off to a bad start. You have a couple of choices. You can continue the way you're going. Or I can help you make a plan. We can't change what happened on the bus. But at lunchtime a friend can go down and help you look for your coat in the bus room, or you can look in the lost and found. I can't make you French toast sticks, but instead of what they had in the cafeteria, would you prefer some crackers?" If a kid is upset, give him a chance to share what's wrong. Show him his choices and help him move on. Otherwise, that kid won't learn a thing all day, because he'll still be stewing about those French toast sticks!

Dear Parents,

Notice the new label on the front of your child's folder. This folder is now known as the <u>Home/School Folder</u>. Each day important papers and notes will be put in this folder to be delivered to you. Please note: One side is labeled "Left at Home" (please take those papers out) and one side is labeled "Bring Right Back" (I need those items returned in the folder). All notes and money from home should also be sent back in the folder. Anything small (e.g., coins, sticky notes) should be placed in the baggie for safe arrival. The Home/School Folder needs to be carried to and from school **each day** in your child's book bag. I will ask the children to bring them to me first thing each morning and will give them back at the end of each day. Please remember to ask to see this folder each night.

Thank you for your support,

today's art project to show your mom, that goes on the left side because you're supposed to leave it at home.

You could tape Ziploc bags inside these folders. I find that if a kid's going to bring lunch money and it's an odd amount, or any other kind of little stuff, it's good if the parent can toss it in the bag. Then it doesn't get lost on the way to school and the kid doesn't get there and start crying because "I don't know where it went!" It's in the Ziploc bag.

If you're a kid in my class, you know I'm going to be at the door when you get to class each morning. You come up to me, and you'd better have your home/school folder in your hand—because if you don't have it in your hand, I'll pretend I don't see you. You hand your folder to me. I have a desk, and as I pull certain things out of the folder, I say, "Oh, lunch money, good; homework, good. Thanks, hon. Good morning. Next one." If somebody has a note from a parent, I see it right away because it's in the home/school folder.

Go straight down the line. Every child who comes in has to hand over her home/school folder. Before I take attendance, it's easy for me to do a quick assessment and say, "I'm missing three. So either three kids are absent today or somebody got by me without a folder." I keep the folders at my desk during the day, and at the end of the day, when the kids get their home/school folders back, that's a signal that we're going to Afternoon Wrap-Up soon.

At the beginning of the year I provide each child with a folder that says "Home/School Folder" right on it, so that there's no "Well, I'm using *this* folder." I learn to recognize the folders, and every folder has on it the name of the child it belongs to.

If you're in my class, you have to have a folder when you leave the room at the end of the day. If you forget your folder, you get one of *my* folders. And my folders talk. They have speech bubbles on them, and every one says, "I belong to Mrs. Whyte. Please return me!" You may borrow it, but you need to bring it back when you find yours at home.

Other teachers use different approaches with the home/school folder. I like the left and right because I think it's one more opportunity to get kids thinking about those words. But the important thing is that however you choose to set up the folders, you need to do it in a way that helps the kids organize their stuff so that they know that's part of the routine.

When Kids Come In at Different Times

In most classrooms, kids don't arrive all at once. They may come in on different buses; they may be part of the breakfast program; they may go to an enrichment program before they get to your class. That's reality. So you need to have a plan for dealing with that time that lets you turn it into learning time even though not everyone is there yet.

This is the time when the kids turn over their home/school folders and get unpacked. After that you might have the kids who get there early start on morning work. If you can use that morning work to reinforce or review what they learned yesterday, or to help them anticipate what's going to happen today, then you've turned that time into learning time.

If you have work stations or centers in your classroom, you might encourage the kids to return to those and finish whatever didn't get done yesterday. You might let them use games or puzzles that are fun but that also help reinforce some basic concepts. Or you might have them work on a thought or a sentence

If They Forget Their Folders

If somebody arrives at school and doesn't have his own folder, you don't give up on that. You don't say, "Okay, well, bring it tomorrow. You'll just have to carry your mail home." This is an important part of our community. If you're in my class, you need to have your folder. If you don't have your folder, then you need to borrow mine, but this is not yours. I put a big speech bubble on it because I used to say to kids, "What's my folder saying?" and then I thought, I'm going to make it talk. "I belong to Mrs. Whyte. I want to go back to her!" Even when the parents see it, they go, "Whoa!" It's your signal to the parents: Find the darned folder! It's our way of communicating.

I remember one kid had four of my folders at home. I finally wrote a note and said, "My folders are speaking to me! It's getting so loud because there's a collection of them! Send them back!"

"THE FOUR Hs"

a handshake,

a hug,

a hand wave,

a high 5.

for Morning Message: "What might we need to write down for Morning Message?" Get them focused on something that will tie into Morning Meeting and what the class is going to be doing that day.

The Signal

Once all the kids have arrived, you need a signal to start Morning Meeting. It can be a bell. It can be clapping in time while chanting "Morning Meeting, Morning Meeting." Or it can be a song. Kids need to know that when the song ends, they should be on the rug for the meeting. They need a few seconds to finish what they're doing. Otherwise you'll get someone like Jeremy, who says, "I was just trying to get that word and now you're bugging me!" They need a signal so that they know they have a couple of seconds to finish up what they're doing and come to Morning Meeting.

You don't have to use the same signal every day. You need to decide: What am I comfortable with? Is it important to my kids this year that the signal always remain the same? Will I get the best results from them if it's always the same? Or can I vary the signal, making it more fun to get there, because the kids can handle that this year? You decide what's best for your class, knowing that what works this year may not be the same thing that worked last year. It all depends on the kids.

Morning Greeting

Now the kids are all on the rug for Morning Meeting. The first thing we do there is greet each other. I think it's really important to get kids talking to other kids, to build that classroom community. It's very hard for a kid to be cruel on the playground to another child he's just shaken hands with and said good morning to. You greeted them at the door, but it's important to have them greet one another, too. I ask every child to greet two other children. I might say, "Look at the person next to you," then "Look at the person in front of you or behind you." Sometimes I tell the kids they can use any one of the "four Hs": a handshake, a hug, a high five, or a hand wave. That gives kids a choice: If I don't want to touch you, I don't have to touch you. I can wave.

If you don't want to use the four Hs, you can use made-up rhymes. I like this one:

Good morning, friend.
Good day to you.
Hope you have fun today
In all you do!

Probably my favorite way of doing Morning Greeting is to turn it into a game I call "Attendance-Go-Round." I bring the attendance cards to Morning Meeting. As soon as everyone is there, I start things off. I might say, "Good morning, Amy." And Amy says, "Good morning, Mrs. Whyte." The kids need to be listening because then I'm going to say, "Good morning, Susan," and Susan isn't going to say, "Good morning, Mrs. Whyte"; she's going to say, "Good morning, Amy." She has to go back to the name of the person before her. Then I say, "Good morning, Michael." And Michael is supposed to say, "Good morning, Susan." We keep going that way until everybody's had a chance. I pick names randomly. I don't go around the circle, so they don't know who's next.

When we play this game, I try to emphasize eye contact because the kids are building relationships. I get some social skills in there, too. If I start off saying, "Good morning, Amy," and Amy says, "Yeah," I say, "No, that's not okay, Amy." I get a chance to correct that kind of social behavior. So then I say, "Good morning, Amy." And she says, "Good morning, Mrs. Whyte."

Songs That Signal "Come to Morning Meeting"

(To the tune of "Row, Row, Row Your Boat")

Come, come, come now,
Time for us to start
Quickly, quickly, quickly, quickly
Join from where you are!

Join, join, join the group
Time for us to start
Quickly, quickly, quickly, quickly
Join from where you are!

(To the tune of "Where is Thumbkin?")

Where are the kids? Where are the kids?
It is time. It is time.
Time for Morning Meeting, time for Morning Meeting!
Join us now. Join us now.

Where is _____? Where is _____?
It is time. It is time.
Time to come on over, time to come on over!
Join us now. Join us now.

(In the last verse of the second song, of course, you insert the name of the last straggler!)

MORNING MESSAGE

After the greeting, all sorts of things can go on in Morning Meeting. Remember the five components of learning—reading, writing, listening, speaking, and viewing information? I figured out that it was pretty easy for me to work every one of those things into Morning Meeting every single day. All I had to do was use an interactive chart. If I used an interactive chart, I could repeat some concepts. I could review what we'd covered the day before. I could assess what the kids had learned and what had gone over their heads. I could introduce new ideas, give them a chance to practice, and extend or enrich concepts they'd already mastered. I could play off it to meet my state standards. And it was fun for the kids!

I like to use a "Morning Message" as my interactive chart during Morning Meeting. I don't know whether you want to write a Morning Message, and I don't want to back you into a corner. Use whatever works for you. If you don't use a Morning Message, maybe instead you share a poem, or there's something already on the chart that you'd like to share. It might be something that you wrote yesterday with the kids, or some familiar story, or maybe a graphic organizer. It just needs to be some kind of interactive chart that you can refer back to.

The important thing is that you take advantage of using that chart time to write for and with the children. You want to read *with* them. You want to read *to* them. And at some point you want to have them read some of it by themselves. The chart gives you a chance to model whatever it is that you want the kids to learn.

Some teachers like to write out a Morning Message ahead of time and then go over it with the kids. I used to do that. For the first few years I taught, I ran into school, got my coffee, ran into the room, and wrote a message as fast as I could—before the kids got there. I was missing a wonderful opportunity to write *with* the children, to give them a model of what writers do when they can't think of something: "I really want to write that word, but I don't know how to spell it. Where am I

A Sample Morning Message at the Beginning of the Year

September 1, 2004

Dear Smarties,

Good morning! Today is Wednesday.

Love,
Mrs. Whyte

going to find out how to spell that word?" When you do it with the kids, you're the model for how they're going to find that information in the classroom.

Another day, maybe I'd model how you get started with writing when you're stuck: "I'm not sure how to start. Well, I know one way to get started is to think about who I'm writing about or what I'm writing about or where something happened." You teach them to think of the five Ws (who, what, when, where, why) or to think about how something happened.

That's why I want a blank piece of paper on that chart when the kids come to Morning Meeting.

Repeat, Repeat, Repeat

So I write the message with the kids. I start with the real little ones in kindergarten and first grade, making it so repetitive that everyone's going to read it successfully. To become readers, they need to *believe* they're readers.

I always start my Morning Message in the same way. I put the date down, and then I write, "Dear Smarties." That's what I call them, and they know that. Every child in my kindergarten

My Favorite Tools

These are some of my favorite tools for Morning Meeting and Afternoon Wrap-Up. You might want to keep them on your tool cart. Children love to use any of these tools, so having them right there is a great way to encourage kids to participate:

- pointers (plastic hands, flyswatters, wands, antennas)
- frames
- eyeglasses with no glass in them (I call them "concentration glasses." They're silly, but they're a great way to get kids to focus.)

- Word Whackers
- highlighting tape
- markers in multiple colors
- white tape for fixing mistakes
- picture clues (see pages 54, 55, 71, 72)

class, once he can write letters, starts writing that word right away. Once the kids have seen it day after day for three or four weeks, every one of them thinks, "Hey, I know how to write that!"—or at least, "I know where to find it." And they copy it—onto whiteboards, onto envelopes. It's important for them to feel that "I know a word. I can write it."

In kindergarten, at the beginning of the year, I write the date and then: "Dear Smarties, Good morning. Today is Tuesday. Love, Mrs. Whyte." That's it! Because I want even the slowest learner in the class to get to two weeks out and say, "I know what it says!" He doesn't know what it says from reading it, but I'll tell you, I remember giving a pointer to this little guy in my class who was not a quick learner. And he came up with that pointer and he said—with absolute confidence—"Dear Smarties, Good morning!" I said, "Michael, hon, look at the words." That's the gift, though. He felt like a reader!

Name That Class!

I call the kids in my class my "Smarties." I started calling them that because I wanted to name them something that they identified with. It's not my classroom. I get to come here every day only because 20-some of you join me. This is our room. The sign on the door says, "Smarties Community, facilitated by Mrs. Whyte." That's what it says because that's my role in there. I want to build a community where kids belong. That's at the heart of good teaching and getting kids to learn.

In my workshops, I often ask teachers to come up with names for their classes. So the teachers make up names, like "Mrs. Green's Googles." I had a teacher who said she called her kids "Mrs. Fulton's Flyers," because she'd tell them, "You're flying today!"

One teacher came up with "Cupcakes." And one of the other teachers was a fourth-grade teacher and she said, "Yeah, I can see me calling mine my cupcakes!" So I said, "What did you come up with?" She said, "I'll call them my dudes—'Mrs. Denning's Dudes.'" And they probably loved that in fourth grade. You need to find what's comfortable for your kids. You might even hold a little classroom survey. Throw out some names and let them vote. Or let them brainstorm and then vote. They take on their own identity.

How to Give Kids "Think Time"

Here's a tool I really like. I call it a time stick. I started with a craft stick, and on one side I glued on a graphic of an alarm clock on red paper. That meant "I'm thinking." Then on the other side I had the alarm clock again, but this time it was on green paper, and it said, "Brrrring!" I told the kids that when they saw the red clock face, they were supposed to sit on their hands and be thinking of

the answer. I'd count a few seconds silently, and then I'd turn the stick and say, "Brrrring!" And then they all could raise their hands to answer. It gave the kids who weren't quite so quick a little time to come up with the answer. You can do the same thing with the reproducibles on page 44.

Code It with Color

Do you know the book *You Read To Me, I'll Read To You*, by MaryAnn Hoberman? I read that book as a volunteer in kindergarten, and it made a huge impression on me. What I loved about it was that even if a child didn't know what it said, he knew when it was his turn to chime in because he saw the colored type. If you're going to write an interactive chart with some repetitive language, like "Run, run, as fast as you can," change the color of the marker you use when you get to that language. Or use highlighting tape to color it. That way every child feels like "Okay, I don't know what the words say, but I know that when she gets to that pink one, I'm going to say, 'Run, run, as fast as you can!'" And then everybody's a part of it, and they all experience success. It's the beginning of tracking print.

In my class, I always wrote "Good morning!" in red. When we were reading the message together and we got to that part, the kids knew to chime in with "Good morning!"

How Much Teaching Can You Get Out of the Date?

I always start with the date at the top, but I write it in different ways. I might start by writing "September 1." Later, I abbreviate the month, and I say, "Do you think Mrs. Whyte's tricking you or did I spell it wrong?" Eventually, I'll use numbers: "9/1/04." And I'll ask the kids, "Did I make a mistake here?"

Some kids will get that in kindergarten. I can still see my Amanda, the kid who was way ahead of everybody else. She came to kindergarten and she was really a second-grade reader. Her mom and dad both worked with her all the time. She knew her way around the library. She'd had more adventures than anybody I knew. *She* told *me* what to do most of the time. And then there was the little one, Nicole. She was on a permanent "in-school field trip": she just wandered around all the time. These two kids

Write with the Kids

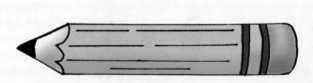

Your Morning Message is something you and the kids write together. You're writing the message, and they're working with you. So when I get to the first line after "Dear Smarties," I say, "What goes here?" And they know. Every morning it says, "Good morning." That's the first thing I write in the body of the letter. So I ask, "What does that start with?"

"A *G*, Mrs. Whyte."

"Oh, a *G*. Where's that letter on the alphabet strip? [I called it the "Smartie line."] Is it in front of the letter *M*? Is it between the letters *F* and *H*?"

Or I say, "Do you know how to write a *G*? Why don't you come here and write it?"

Later in the year, after they've mastered the part that's repeated every day, we extend Morning Message. I might say, ""We're going to talk about what the student teacher might do today." (They know that the student teacher is really the student helper, and that it's a different child every day.) Or I might say, "Who can help me remember what our special is today?" Or "What are we maybe going to be doing today? Making pancakes? Let's write about making pancakes." They're learning to extend the message, and they're also learning to look ahead and anticipate what might happen later in the day.

were so different in their abilities to take in information. Amanda would be considered gifted and talented. Nicole would be considered the slow learner in the class. They both benefited from coming to Morning Meeting and watching me write the date in our Morning Message.

Within a week, Amanda had "gotten it" that I was using an abbreviation for the month. She knew it; she whipped it off; she'd mastered it. It was going to take Nicole a lot longer to figure out that I could write it either way. We never know when something's going to click for kids. What we need to do is keep putting it out there. It will click when they're ready for it to click, but we need to keep offering those basic concepts.

So those are the starting points. Every day I'd repeat the date, the greeting, the "Good morning!" and the day of the week. You may want to focus on different things. You may want to use a different format. Do whatever works for you and your kids. Just keep it simple in the beginning, and keep repeating things, so that all the kids can succeed.

One day you might use Morning Message to model where you start on the paper when you're writing: "Oh, my goodness, where do I start? Well, maybe I can think about where we start to read in a book. We start at the top of the page, all the way at the left side. Maybe I'll try starting there when I write, too."

Fun (!) with Standards

I think that sometimes teachers get a little overwhelmed with the idea of a Morning Message because there are so many things you can do with it. They're not sure where to go next. I always tell teachers, "Don't try to focus on everything all at once." If you're not sure exactly what you want to include in your Morning Message, take another look at the standards for your state. Think about directionality. Think about punctuation. Think about spacing. Go through the list of standards and think, "How could I get at that in a Morning Meeting chart?" Make a list for yourself that shows the standards for your state and how you're playing off different ones in each day's Morning Message. Always play off the basics that are part of the standards.

Take spacing, for example. Morning Message gives you a wonderful opportunity to teach spacing. Just jam your words together as you write the message, and then start saying them that way. Maybe you're writing about the student teacher in Morning Message. When you write the interactive chart in the morning, the kids

The Pieces of Morning Meeting

I can't give you a schedule for Morning Meeting. I'm not in your school or in your class. I don't know your style or what your children need. And I sure don't know the interruptions you have! But I can give you an outline of what worked for me. This is just a starting point. The blank lines are included because I would encourage you to add to it whatever you can use to introduce concepts to your kids, and to let them practice, extend, and master those concepts.

Morning Greeting
Morning Message or other
    interactive chart
Announcements
Song
Schedule
Calendar
Interactive bulletin boards
_____
_____

might say to you, "Molly's the student teacher today." So you start writing that. And you say, "Oh, boy, sometimes when I start writing, I really get going and it gets a little messy. Oh, no. What's the problem with this? I don't even know where my words begin or end, do I? How am I going to read it? I don't know whether the *S* goes with the *T* or what. How would I know that?"

You can do it in a fun way. If I see a kid cramming his letters together during journal time, then the next morning, in Morning Meeting, I'll cram my words together and say, "Well, you guys think *I* can read that. Why can't *you* read it?" Or I might write something and then say, "Go ahead and read it." It's just modeling the same thing that they did. "Well, why can't we do that? Because then no one else can read it."

You can work on punctuation in Morning Message, too. If you use quotation marks every day to identify what somebody said, chances are you won't ever have to teach a formal lesson on quotation marks. The kids start to use them because they see *you* use them. You might say, "Well, when somebody says something, we put that in what today? Quotes." Put them up there and you'll be amazed: if you say something often enough, you'll see the kids starting to get it. When you repeat for the kids and you model for them, you give everybody a chance. To me, that's so much better than saying, "I taught quotes the 3rd of October, and I guess some kids didn't get them. . . ."

Morning Message is also a great place to teach directionality. Some of our little kindergarteners need to hear you say, "You start at the top—this is the top of the paper." It's important to say those words out loud. Say, "This is the top," instead of just

Other Standards You Can Address with Interactive Charts

Here are just a few of the things that may be on your state's list of standards. Any of them can be practiced, enriched, maintained, and mastered by your kids if you write with the kids and for them every day during Morning Meeting:

- consonants and vowels
- sounds (beginning and ending sounds, blends, and digraphs)
- directionality
- punctuation
- letters, words, sentences, and symbols
- spacing
- sight words
- rhyming
- friendly letter format
- contractions
- compound words
- root words, prefixes, and suffixes
- synonyms, antonyms, and homonyms

All states require that students be able to identify the letters of the alphabet. So maybe one day in Morning Meeting, you circle individual letters on your interactive chart and you ask the kids to identify them. Reading and writing standards require that kids be able to recognize and sort capital and lowercase letters. So maybe another day you put an X under every capital letter. Or you ask the kids to do it. And you ask them to underline the lowercase letters.

Another day, maybe you have children point out different punctuation marks. Or you address the standard that says students will be able to read words by sounding out and blending their separate sounds.

We can look for sounds; we can also work on syllables. You might include a longer word in your Morning Message. Then say, "Let's take this word apart." And you show the kids how to break *au/to/mo/bile* into syllables, so that they can figure out the word.

starting. Model it for them. And then, to teach directionality, say, "You know, we always go this way. I was thinking today, maybe I'll read it this way instead." Try to say it as though you're reading right to left. "Wait a minute, guys. This is terrible. I can't read it. What's the problem?" Well, the problem is that writing goes left to right, not right to left. Take those opportunities to say that out loud, so that directionality becomes just a natural part of writing and reading.

That's such a quick lesson, but some of those kids are going to kick in with that. The next day you reinforce that: "Where do we start? Oh, we start at the top, that's right. Let's get the marker up here. Does everyone know where we start?"

Everyone won't always get it right away. But the more we talk about directionality, the sooner they figure out what it is. "Notice I start right here when I write our Morning Message. Why do I start at the top? Why don't I start down here, at the bottom?" Someone will say it. Someone might get it. Someone might not. We're going to say it again many times throughout the time that we write together. That will give everyone the chance to get it.

You're not always the one deciding what to write. Sometimes the kids decide, and you just facilitate: "Does anyone have something to share on our chart? Can anyone think of something we might do today?"

"We're gonna have recess."

"Well, give me more. What might you do at recess today? Maybe we could add that to the chart."

Make the Message Match the Need

So you start off with the very basic message, you keep repeating it, and you figure out how you can play off the message to meet your state standards. Now there's another layer you can add. I'm always trying to play off what they did get, what they didn't get, or what we just need to review, review, review—or extend or enrich. Sometimes the message is secondary. Whatever it is that I need to get across to them, that's what the message becomes.

Maybe I taught this great lesson—what I *thought* was a wonderful lesson—on compound words yesterday, but by Afternoon Wrap-Up I realize nobody got it. That means the next morning I'm going to put those compound words in my message somewhere. So I have to fake it and say, "You know, I think I could write about . . . Ooh, I think I saw a rainbow near the railroad tracks on my way to school. Maybe I'll write about the rainbow. Can anybody help Mrs. Whyte? What could I say?" That's my job: to figure out how to bring in whatever I need to get across and make it seem as though it's just kind of flowing into the message. The kids might say, "Rainbows are pretty."

Take sight words. You can use Morning Message to reinforce words the class is working on. Try leaving out one of those words in Morning Message. Write the message without using the word *the* and show the kids what happens. Or see how often the same word can be included in a paragraph without sounding silly.

Sometimes I'd leave a blank and say, "Gee, I don't remember how to spell that word. How do you think I could find out how to spell it?" And the kids would say, "You have to look on the word wall!" Then later on in writing, when a child would come to me and say, "I don't know how to spell it," I'd say, "Gee we did that this morning in Morning Meeting. Where are you going to find it? How are you going to solve that problem?" I was training them in problem-solving—showing them what to do when they didn't know the answer.

Conventional wisdom has it that 100 words make up 50 percent of what we read and write every day. My kids need to know those 100 words. That's always been a huge issue for me.

For the Days When This All Seems Overwhelming

One teacher said to me, "Donna, you think too fast on your feet. I couldn't sit there and think of a lesson off the top of my head." But I remember telling her, "I think you're going way too deep. I think you're thinking you need some extravagant lesson. What you need to know is standards. What are my school standards and what are my state standards?"

Standards are given to us every year. If one of them says that I will teach kids capital letters, then every once in a while when we're writing our Morning Message, I'll talk about capital letters. I don't ever "teach capital letters" because I teach them every time I refer to a chart or some other material.

I think sometimes we get too hung up on "What's the lesson?" Sometimes we don't need an elaborate lesson plan. Sometimes we need to recognize whether children are with us and just play off what's going on at that "teachable moment."

I've always felt that there are certain basic words and if kids could master just those words, they'd feel as though they could read. So I want to look for opportunities to say, "Hey, has anybody seen this word before? It happens to be one of our sight words this week. Where would I find it if I didn't know how to spell it?"

When you do this, you're teaching more than just sight words. You're teaching more than problem-solving skills. You're modeling writing by describing what you're doing, thinking, and using to be a good writer. When kids see and hear an adult write, they begin to get the connection between the written word and oral language. They're observing concepts about print firsthand. That's how they learn what it means to be a good writer.

How Do You Build Sight-Word Vocabulary?

On the road one year I did a little impromptu survey of teachers from kindergarten through second grade and I was amazed: around the United States, they were being asked to teach anywhere from zero to 300 sight words. Three hundred sight words—that's a lot! But if you have to teach that many, I think there's a better way than having kids memorize flash cards. I think you can concentrate on exposing kids to those words all the time. You can use Morning Message to build visual recognition by exposure, to show kids how often those words appear—maybe even by using a highlighter or highlighting tape. Ask the kids to come show you which words in the Morning Message are sight words you're working on. There's so much opportunity for those words to keep popping up. We need to take advantage of those opportunities.

I like to use "popcorn words" to expose kids to sight words. Popcorn words are easy. Make several copies of the reproducible on page 52. For each one, cut out the part that's inside the outline, and put a piece of yellow cellophane behind the outline. Then just keep putting that "popcorn" over individual words in your Morning Message— or anywhere else in the room—so that they keep "popping up." You can make sure that at least five of the words for the week are highlighted every day in Morning Message. You can highlight the popcorn words yourself, or you can have the kids do it. You want the kids to see that those important sight words really are all around them.

Pictures Help Them "Read" the Words

When the kids are young, I like to include visual clues in our Morning Message. If the message says, "Today we are going to paint," put a picture of a paint can and paintbrushes next to the word *paint*. (Use the reproducibles on pages 54, 55, 71, and 72 and attach them to the message with ticky-tack or double-sided tape.) Have the students "read" the message. I might say, "We are going to . . . What are we going to do today?"

"Paint!"

"Right! How did you know that was *paint*?" The picture gives a clue to the word.

If, instead of paint, I'd used a picture of crayons, then the kids would have known that we were going to color. The picture gives them the clue. You're going to take advantage of those opportunities over and over again. And you hope that eventually, when they get to reading group, they're going to recognize that "Oh, yeah—the picture matches the word." Eventually.

It's even neater, if you're trying to connect picture and word, to write the word beneath the picture. And eventually you get to the point where you say, "What if I take the picture away? Bet you don't know what it says now!"

"Paint!"

"How'd you know?" They remember the picture, and there's the word.

As the year goes on, sometimes Morning Message will include some kind of direction. Maybe in the message you'll say, "Today we're going to cut out our pumpkins." When that happens, include the picture clue, because the chart stays up all day. Some child is going to forget that direction, but he'll be able to look back and see the picture. So I tell my kids, "When we get to Afternoon Wrap-Up, if I ask you about Morning Message, what should you do if you don't know? Don't say, 'I don't know!' Just look up there and figure it out. And then you'll have the answer." You're teaching them to look back at a resource to get the answer.

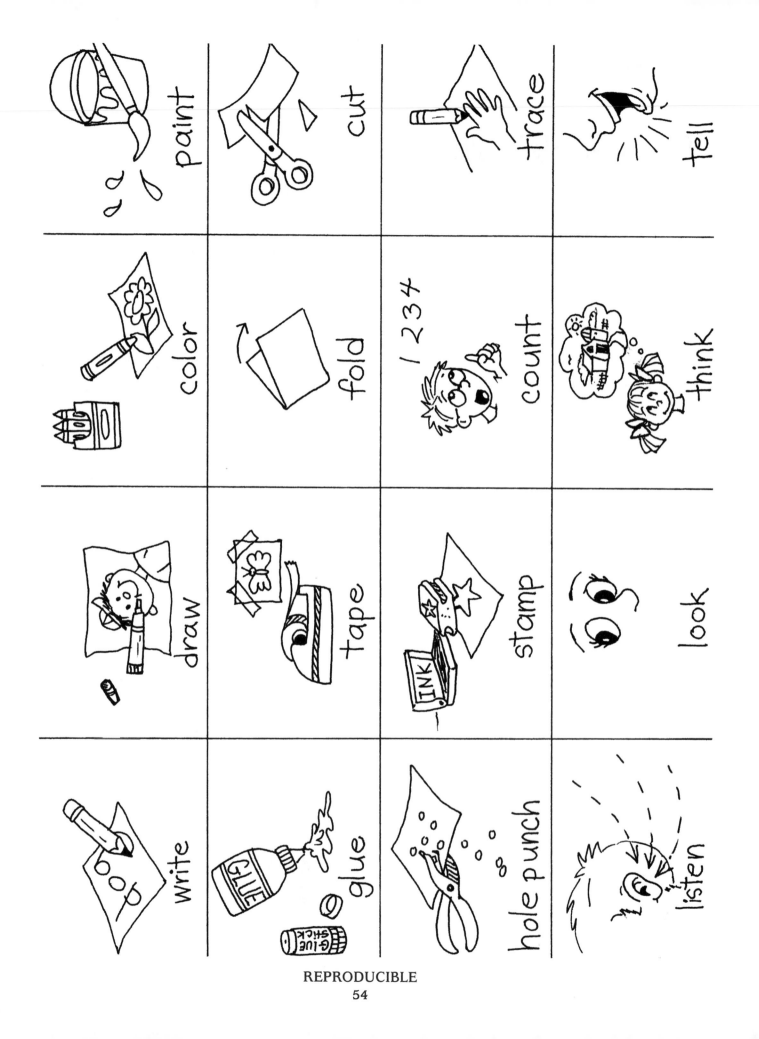

paint

cut

trace

tell

color

fold

count

think

draw

tape

stamp

look

write

glue

hole punch

listen

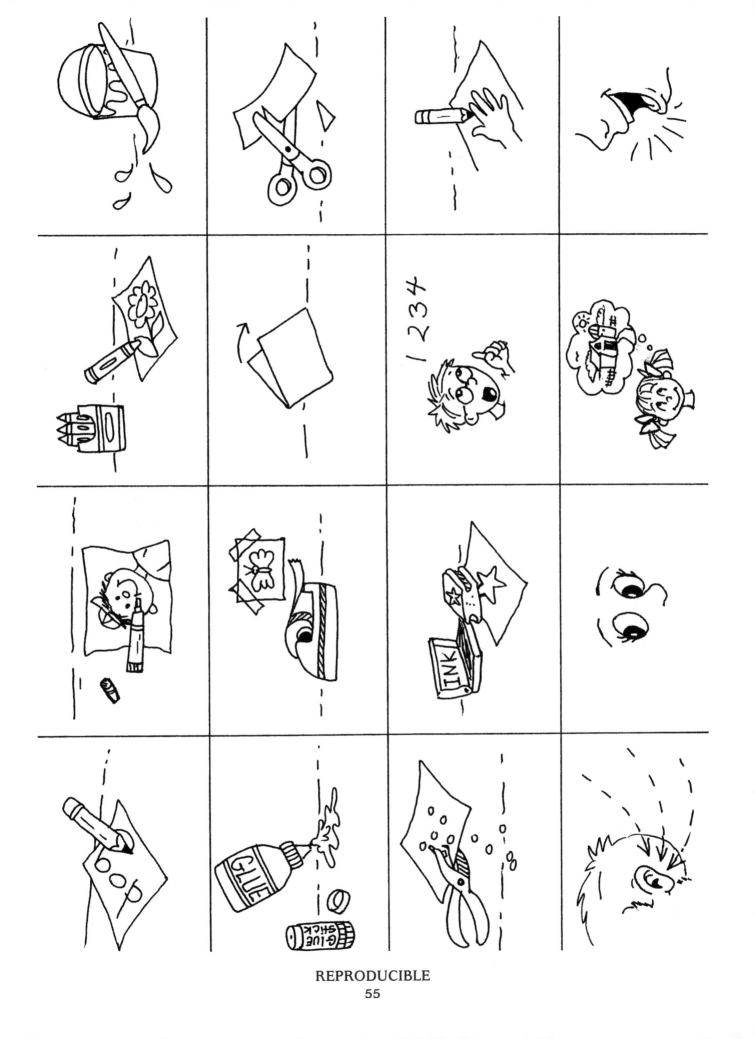

Make Mistakes!

Did the teecher make a mistake?

Later on in the year, you can make mistakes. Kids love it when you make mistakes. I always blame it on the coffee. I say, "You know, Mrs. Whyte didn't have her second cup of coffee, and I think I might have made a mistake here. Does anyone see any problems with this message?" The kids will start to pick them out. It's important for them to see how language looks.

You might write *teecher* and say, "Why isn't this *teacher*? We learned yesterday that *ee* sounds like this. Why isn't it *teecher*? It looks like *teacher* to me!" But it just doesn't happen to be the way that particular word is spelled. It doesn't follow that rule you set. So you want to point that out.

Some teachers tell me they don't want to write an interactive chart in front of the kids. They're worried about what would happen if they made a mistake and had to start over. But what's the message you're sending to the kids then? I think if you make a mistake, you should have white Post-it notes or some of that big white tape that comes from the dollar store— somebody referred to it once as "boo-boo tape"—and you should say, "Oh! Giant white-out!" Just stick that tape on there and write over the mistake.

That's such an important message that you can send to kids. Model what you do when you make a mistake. They can learn just from the fact that you're willing to admit it: "We need the giant white-out here!" And then you tape it on top, and you write over it and say, "I'm so glad I wasn't whining about that! Whining wouldn't have solved this problem!" Don't be surprised if, during a writing center or journal time, someone asks for the boo-boo tape!

Then the next time you make a mistake, maybe you do whine. You say, "Awwww, guys. See what Mrs. Whyte did? Now I'll just quit!" Use a whiny voice. And they'll laugh at you, but then you say, "That's what you guys sound like sometimes! So what am I going to do instead? I'm not going to whine about it. Just get the roll of giant white-out!"

What If They Don't Find the Mistakes?

Sometimes you can make a mistake without pointing it out to the kids. You're hoping that someone will identify it. But what if they don't?

Don't sweat it! You're trying to challenge the learners who can go there, who can spot the mistakes and learn from them. But if they don't all get there, don't worry about it. Just try it again another day.

Are You Including Everyone?

My biggest concern is the kids who are left out. Research shows that when you talk to a group of kids, you generally can plan on some of the group taking in what you say. They understand it, and they're actually paying attention. That's the top 2 percent. Then you have this middle group: they do understand it, but they're not really paying attention. So some of it goes in; some of it goes out; it's kind of a mishmash. That's the whole bell curve in the middle. Then there are these little guys at the other end: They might even be looking at you and smiling. They're not listening to a darned thing you say. The reality is that they're over there in their own little world.

Questioning kids works the same way. Across the United States, we've been leaving kids out. I've been in many classrooms where I've heard teachers doing what I did until a mentor teacher mentioned it to me. I left kids out—never on purpose, never meaning to, but I didn't think about it. I left them out because I pointed to the writing and said things like "Who can find the sight words on this interactive chart?"

Well, I'm very sorry, Amy. You don't even know what a sight word is. You call them "word-wall words," so when I change it to "sight words," you don't know what I'm asking for. So you don't raise your hand. You, Christopher, know one sight word, but it's not the one on the chart. So you're looking as though you don't know any because you can't identify any of the ones on my chart. Nathan knows sight words but he doesn't talk, so he's not going to raise his hand. It's not in his personality. And Jennifer is the show-off. She's got her hand up. She knows every sight word on there. She can read the whole chart. But she doesn't need to—because Jennifer is the kid in the 2 percent. She's the only one I really included.

We assume, "Gee, they got all the directions. I *gave* them those directions." But it's not that simple.

I think of my Michael. One day I sat with him at a center. I was trying very hard to get him to focus, and I said, "Michael, do you get it, hon?"

He said, "Yes."

I said, "Then repeat it back to me."

And he said, "What's that in your teeth?"

He didn't get it because that's not where his focus was—it wasn't on the words. So we have to be careful of that, remembering that some of them are going to pick up some of what we say, and very few are going to get all of it.

If I change the way I question the kids in my classroom, I open the lesson up to all of the children. I need to be cautious with close-ended questions. I need to say things like "Hey, guys, what do you notice about Mrs. Whyte's chart today?" Everybody's invited. If a child is quiet, I might need to call on him and recognize that. But when you put it in that language, you'll be surprised. When I started doing it, part of me was always thinking, "Oh, my gosh, am I gonna get through this day?" But you'd be amazed what a difference the language makes. It invites kids into the community instead of pushing them out.

So I want to take those opportunities to question kids in a way that opens it up to them.

The first time I ever said, "What do you notice about this chart?" little Ryan raised his hand. Ryan was never one of the kids in that top 2 percent, so I was thinking, "What did Ryan notice?"

And he said, "I noticed it's a little messy."

"It's messy? Ryan, what's messy?" What you need to do as a teacher is say, "How do I take what he just said and turn it into my next lesson?"

My next lesson was "What's messy? The top? Or the bottom?" (Point to those parts of the chart as you say the words.)

"The bottom, Mrs. Whyte."

I'd been sitting in a chair and writing, and in fact, when I got to this part of the chart, I did kind of go off to the side. So I knew which part he thought was messy. But I said, "Is it a word? Or is it the whole sentence that you think is messy?"

He said, "Just the end."

I said, "So it's this word. Do you know what this word is?" You can play off what they say, no matter what it is, to teach them something else.

You can get into trouble with this. You'd better be on your toes. I had a name wall in my classroom that had all of the kids' names on it. We played off kids' names—kids love that. We'd count the letters, compare who had how many letters, who had which sound at the beginning, what their names ended with. I sent Ryan to the word wall during Morning Meeting one day, and I said, "Ryan, bring me two names that are different—not the same, different." And he came back with the names *Katy* and *Cody*.

Then I thought, "How are these two names different? Okay, they both have four letters. Ryan's that kid who doesn't really know his letters yet, so it's not the letters and sounds that he's looking at. He must be counting the letters. But they have the same number of letters, so it can't be that. What could it be? I'm thinking he's going to say something about the first letter of each name. I just know it."

The easy way to find out what he was thinking was just to say, "Ryan, how are these two names different?" And he said, "One's a girl and one's a boy." That was true—there were little pictures on the cards. He didn't even look at the words—he looked at the pictures. He knew one was a girl and one was a boy, and he brought back those names. Then I said, "Yes. And notice there's a *y* in each name, and there are four letters in each name. And even though one starts with *C* and one starts with *K*, they sound similar."

Could I teach off it? Yes. Was it what I was expecting? Absolutely not.

Now, I sent Ryan back to the word wall that day. I said, "This time, Ryan, when you come back, I want to see two names that are the same. Okay? Ryan, give it to me. Not different. The same." And he came back. This time the two names were *Jeremiah* and *Ann*. What was the same about those two names? I thought, "It has to be the *A*. If he recognizes a

Questioning Kids

When you get kids to discover a concept for themselves, they hang onto it. They think they discovered it. But you've got to get them there by asking the right questions. Here are some to try:

- What do you notice?
- Can anyone tell me anything about this _____?
- Does anything on the chart/in the picture/in the writing make you think of something in your life?

- What part did you spot?
- What do you think?
- Do you see something _____ (different, familiar, weird, etc.)?
- What do you recognize?
- Can you tell me what you see?
- Can you show me something on the chart?
- What do you know about this (chart, calendar, book)?
- Does anyone have any ideas about _____?

capital versus a lowercase *A*, he must be looking at the *A*." If I wanted to know, I had to ask him, "Ryan, how are these two names the same?" He said, "I don't like either one of those names."

"Why don't you like those names, Ryan?"

"Because *Jeremiah* takes too long to write, and *Ann* is no fun because it only has three letters."

You have to be prepared for the answers. You need to be able to teach off those, and sometimes it's tough. How are you going to teach off that? I'm riding a plane that involves letters, sounds, number of sounds. He's on a different plane. He's going in a different direction. I need to then take what he says and figure out how I can turn it into a lesson. So I might then say, "Ryan, Jeremiah's

A Sample Morning Message from Later in the Year

When the kids get into the routine of it, the message starts to get longer. By December, you might have a message that looks like the one at the right.

The kids put their guesses, with their names, at the bottom of the chart. Just before the special guest gets there, take a look at the chart and see if anybody guessed the answer.

Maybe this is a day that we look at vocabulary in the message. "What do we really mean when we say 'a week has flown by'?"

Another day, maybe somebody has a new baby in the family. So I might write, "Five kids is a big family. How many kids are in your family?" Here again, each child would write at the bottom of the chart. Each one would write the number of kids in his family and then write his name next to the number. So I have a chance to address the "most common number" in our class's families or the "smallest number versus the largest number" of people in a family.

> Dec. 10, 2004
>
> Dear Smarties,
>
> Good morning! Today is Friday. Our week sure has flown by. We have a special visitor coming at 2 o'clock. I wonder if a Smartie can guess who it is. Write your guess below. Don't forget your name.
>
> Love,
> Mrs. Whyte
>
> Grandma—Heather
> the fire chief—Joe
> the librarian—Nathan

name has a lot of sounds in it. When there are a lot of sounds, there are a lot of letters. Can you help me count how many letters each name has?"

By then Ann is crying, "He doesn't like my name!" So that might turn into its own lesson. But the reality is, we don't know what's in kids' heads. And so the way we question them is really important. I think the way we question kids in Morning Meeting and Afternoon Wrap-Up is huge.

How Long Is Long Enough?

Most of the time, Morning Message takes about five or ten minutes. You have time only to touch on the things we've been talking about. But once you get the kids involved, it can be great. One teacher in Alaska told me, "Donna, one day I spent an hour and 10 minutes on the message. We wrote four pages. Everyone kept adding things." If you can get that much teaching out of it, and the kids stay with you, I'd keep going. The minute you start to lose them, cut the message short. It's time to add the period and move on. Maybe it's time for a song or a chant or getting them up to hop for a minute or whatever it is. You need to give them time in between. If they're with you, stay with it. If they're not, then go on to something else.

If you wonder whether Morning Meeting is worth the time you're taking for it, just list all the opportunities to teach that you found in that interactive chart today. Look at the skills you taught and think to yourself, "Was it time well spent?" When I said that to the teacher in Alaska, she came back with 18 things that she had covered by playing off this chart. I said to her, "If you can do that, then I think you spent your time well, babe. You probably did more than some people do in five hours."

A Quick Tip

During Morning Meeting, kids love to come up to the interactive chart and point out something they've noticed. They love it even more if you give them special pointers. Let them use decorated "hands," "Word Whackers," mini-pointers, holiday erasers on the ends of dowels—anything that will make it fun to get up and point something out. (If you love these things as much as I do, check out the Web site for Crystal Springs Books: www.crystalsprings.com. They have all kinds of this stuff.)

The "Me" Folder

We need to understand that kids are coming to school with "me" folders. It's all about "me." It really is, when you're little. If it's not about you, then you want to know, "How is it related to me?" To a little kid, if it's not about me, it's probably not important. We need to build on the "me" folder and get them thinking in broader terms about "How do these things that I'm learning tie into me?" Always try to play off that. So in Morning Message, write about what they'll do, or where they'll go, or how they'll make something. Keep it personal. The more Morning Message is about them, or they see their own names in it, the more you're going to connect with them.

Include the Student Teacher

One way to get kids' names into Morning Message is to always include something about the student teacher—the student whose turn it is to take care of all the little jobs in the classroom that day. Other people might call him a student helper.

The student teacher is pretty important, so I want to be sure to include his name in our Morning Message. I might just write, "Today the student teacher is James." Or I might say, "James will be at the student teacher's desk today." Or "James will be choosing a partner to help." Or "Who will be the student teacher?" Use any of these last three and you've taught the two words *will* and *be*, and if you use the last one, you've taught questions as well.

At the end of the day, the student teacher takes our Morning Message home—that's why I like to use chart paper instead of writing the message on the board. And I'm hoping that it becomes interactive reading for the parents and the kid. The kids love it. They say, "That's my chart today."

At some point in first grade, the student teacher is even the message writer. The kids love doing this. They see it as a special privilege. You don't even have to give them any direction. You'll be surprised when you see them model what you've been doing all along. Sometimes it can be pretty funny when they start imitating you! But often the student teacher will get to the chart even before you get there and will start to model the repetitive parts of the message on her own. Then you can facilitate the rest. You can ask a question. You can say, "What book do you think we might finish reading today?" Then say, "Do you want to write that or do you want me to help?"

Connecting Writing and Reading

Don't ever make the mistake of writing the whole chart without going back and rereading it at the end. Find the time to reread the chart. People don't write and leave it. Good writers go back. Now that it's written, it's time for you to read it in its entirety. Or have the children read it in its entirety. You need to connect that reading and writing. You're still modeling good writing. And reading back through the message also builds verbal skills and listening skills. Think about the importance of editing any writing you do, and use this opportunity to teach that editing.

Some Hints for Writing with Children

I think Morning Message can be a wonderful tool for teaching children. Here's a quick checklist of things you can do to include everyone:

- Give color clues. Let them see that "Good morning" is always in red.

- Make some parts that are the same every single day. Always begin with the date, the same greeting, and the same one or two sentences.

- Play off sight words. Find a way to work some of this week's words into Morning Message.

- Remember the "me" message. Kids respond best when the message includes something they can relate to.

- Print neatly and skip lines. Make it easy for kids to read the message.

- Follow a friendly letter format. Include the date, and vary the style for the date.

- Use picture clues. Help them learn to associate the picture with the word.

- Don't make promises for events. Say, "We plan to . . . ," not "We will . . ."

- Keep questions open. Let kids show what they do know instead of focusing on what they don't know.

- Make mistakes. Model how to deal with a mistake.

- Leave blanks for the kids to fill in. Let them figure out where they can look for the answers.

Dealing with School Announcements

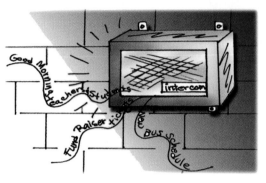

Often, it's during Morning Meeting that someone from the principal's office comes over the intercom with announcements for the whole school. Make sure you have a plan for dealing with that, because that first year those announcements are a headache. You don't always know when they're going to come. You don't know how long they're going to last. So what's your plan for dealing with them? Are you going to incorporate them into Morning Meeting? Are you going to wait to start Morning Meeting until the announcements are over? You need a plan.

My plan was always this: I knew that morning announcements would come during Morning Meeting. It might be while a kid was talking; it might be while I was talking. So I told the kids that as soon as they heard that bell, they needed to "freeze." And I'd model that—I'd show them what it meant to freeze.

I think the sad thing is, kids don't really hear what that person on the intercom is saying. So make it a part of Morning Message. Maybe there's nothing important in the announcements. Maybe Mrs. Fletcher says, "Good morning. There will be no soccer practice today." That doesn't even involve us, so it doesn't go to the "me" message. But what if she says, "Mrs. Green is out, and there's no substitute, so there won't be any library today"? That's an important piece of information for us. We need to take in that information and then we need to say, "Well, where do we file information that we hear coming in?"

If it involves your kids, you might even say, "Well, I know what my next sentence is going to be! 'Mrs. Green is not in school today!'" Then it becomes a creative writing exercise to say, "Where is Mrs. Green today? I bet I know where Mrs. Green is." And I laugh about it. And then the kids write about where they think Mrs. Green is. They think she's out to lunch, eating Chinese.

YOU GOTTA HAVE MOVEMENT!

Never forget that if you want this meeting to hold, you'd better figure out how you're going to move the kids every once in a while. You can't expect kids to sit all the time. In educational circles, you always hear different theories about how long kids can sit still. Many people go by the rule of thumb that the average attention span of a child is his age plus 3 minutes.

That's the *average* child. Now let's talk about the child who's not average. Maybe he came to school at age 4. Instead of saying he can sit still for his age plus 3 minutes, you might as well call it his age minus 3, because he's not average. That means you have 1 minute to give that child direction.

Then you've got the kids at the other end. They're not average either. Let's say one of these kids is 6. If you add 3, that means you have 9 minutes. But in reality, this child could be good for 20 to 25 minutes if you have something that really interests him.

So you can pick whatever rule of thumb you like. The bottom line is, there's no way you can expect a bunch of kids to sit quietly all morning and still be learning anything. If I use the "age plus 3" rule and the kids in my class are 5, I've got 8 minutes. If I've already used 10 on the interactive chart, I'm beyond time. I'd better move them. Now.

This is when you need a song, a poem, a chant—anything to get the kids moving. Every teacher I know has a collection of these. You can use "The Hokey Pokey" or "The Farmer in the Dell." Or you can use an old tune and have the whole class make up new words for it together. It doesn't matter where you get this stuff. I like to keep a file box of the class's favorite songs and poems. Then when the kids need some physical activity, I pick a song or poem out of the file box and we sing or say it together. Or I let the kids pick a favorite. Ideally, we sing a song that involves movement. But even if we're just singing "Old MacDonald," I want them at least to be standing while they sing. I've gotta get them standing up for a few minutes!

One of My Favorite Songs

Here's a song/poem I especially like, and kids seem to like it too. It's called "Popcorn." It's from my CD *Dinosaurs, Popcorn, Penguins, and More.* The chorus is sung to the tune of "Shoo, Fly, Don't Bother Me." Kids can recite the rest of the words and do the movements at the same time.

POPCORN

CHORUS

Popcorn, please pop for me.
   Popcorn, please pop for me.
   Popcorn, please pop for me,
   Pop, pop, popcorn

Tap your right foot,
   Now your left foot.
   Tap both those feet.
Pop, pop, popcorn
Twist your waist.
   Come on, do the twist.
   Get your arms going.
   Pop, pop, popcorn
Arms up high,
   Arms down low,
   Arms out front,
   Pop, pop, popcorn
Rub your belly.
   Tap your head.
   Try to do both.
   Pop, pop, popcorn

CHORUS

Grab your right knee.
   Grab your left knee.
   Cross over.
   Pop, pop, popcorn
Jump forward.
   Jump backward.
   Jump up and down.
   Pop, pop, popcorn
Turn this way.
   Turn that way.
   Spin yourself around,
   Pop, pop, popcorn
Let's spin again,
   One more time.
   Are you feeling dizzy?
   Pop, pop, popcorn
Touch your toes.
   Touch your nose.
   Can you touch both?
   Pop, pop, popcorn

CHORUS repeats twice

THE SCHEDULE

So you've done Morning Message. You've gotten them moving with a song, and now the kids are ready to move on. They need a change of pace. They also need to know what's going to happen: "Where am I going to be today?" This is when you get to the schedule for the day. The schedule gives you a way to let kids know what to expect, what to prepare for, what to look forward to. They like that.

The schedule is actually a pocket chart. You can buy them ready-made or make your own. You can use analog "clocks" or you can make little clock faces with the hands on them. Or use the reproducible on page 69. However you choose to handle the mechanics, the schedule gives you a great way to teach time every day.

I made my own pocket-chart schedule, and I made the cards to go in the pockets. It worked like this: We said, okay, around this time we're going to be in Morning Meeting. Then we had centers, and after that we had a remedial math teacher. So math had to start when the remedial math teacher came, which meant that math would start at 11. I wanted to make the clock with the little hands show that math was going to begin at 11. That way, a kid in the back of the room working in his centers could look at the clock and say, "Uh-oh, I'm going to run out of time here."

I can teach the kids to do that: I can teach them to know what the next thing is on the schedule. I can show them about what

Changing the Schedule? Warn Those Kids!

If you're going to change the schedule from your usual routine, you'd better let the kids know first thing in the morning. In my class, Caitlin was one of those kids. She knew what time lunch was, and if you traded lunch with any other teacher, you'd better let her know, because if she didn't know, she was going to wig out when that time came.

Kids need, just as we do, a warning about what's going to happen. It's especially good to forewarn those kids who depend on continuity. Always remember to allow for that.

time it starts. I can show them how to watch for that time on the big classroom clock. I remember sticking highlighting tape on that clock and saying, "When the big hand hits that highlighting tape, you're going to be out of time. So you need to keep track of that hand up there." You're teaching them the beginnings of managing time.

Telling Time

In every grade from kindergarten through fourth grade, children need to have a chance to practice telling time. Is it going to be one week in February? Or is it going to be anytime you can bring it up? Make this practice work for you and the kids. Maybe today I don't have time in Morning Meeting. I'd love to touch on time, but today I'm working on a couple of other things I have to practice, so I'm just going to tell the kids, "This is today's schedule, and you'll note that there's a change right here." I'm not going to refer to the clock.

Other days, when I have the opportunity, I'm going to say, "Why would that big hand be past the 12 like that? Oh, because we're not going to go there until five minutes after." You take that opportunity to teach them how to tell time, and the language and vocabulary of time.

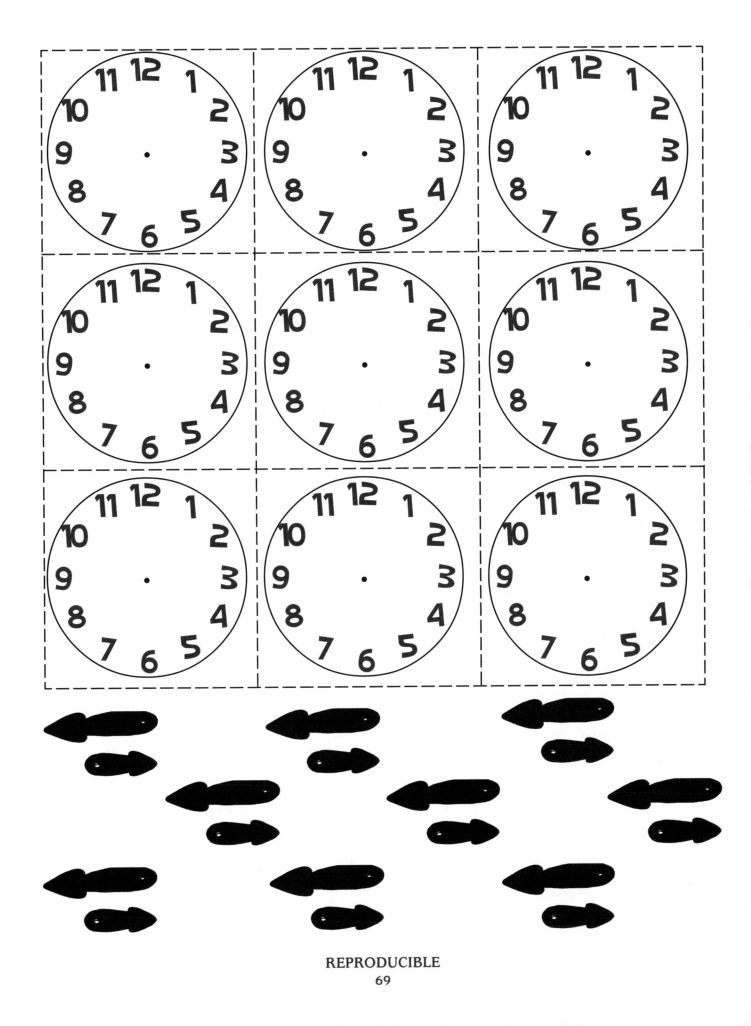

Another Chance to Use Picture Clues

You can use picture clues in the schedule just as you did in Morning Message. Just make copies of the reproducibles on page 71. Use these clues to show that you're celebrating somebody's birthday (the birthday cake), or that this is music time (a musical staff) or reading time (a book), or that you have an assembly today (the microphone). It's one more chance to let kids feel like real readers. Reading pictures is that first step.

But You Promised!

You do have to be careful about how you present the schedule. Never physically write a promise like "Today we're having an assembly" or "Today we're going to . . ." because if that doesn't come true, that's enough to set a little kid off. "You said we were!" Can't you just hear them?

I make sure the kids understand what I mean when I write, "We're supposed to go to an assembly at 2 o'clock." That way they realize that sometimes we say things in certain ways. It doesn't mean we're promising. We're just saying that that's what we expect to do: "I'm going to give you the schedule today, and as much as I can, I'm going to stick to that schedule. But if something comes up and I don't get to it, sweetie, it's not that I made a promise that I broke. I just didn't get to it. So let me just tell you that this is a tentative schedule. This is what we *might* do today, and I hope we'll get to everything." Be careful with your wording because kids take it very literally once you've written it down, and they'll hold you to what to them is a promise.

You give kids a format to follow: "Yes, we're going to have to move on." Just make sure you do it without making promises.

Sometimes the schedule in my classroom didn't say that we were going to have math at 11. Sometimes it just said that we were going to be doing centers for 20 minutes. So the kids had to figure out how long that was and how much time they had left. Use warning signals to remind them to check the time. Maybe you clap, or use rain sticks, or flick the lights. That helps them get the concept of time.

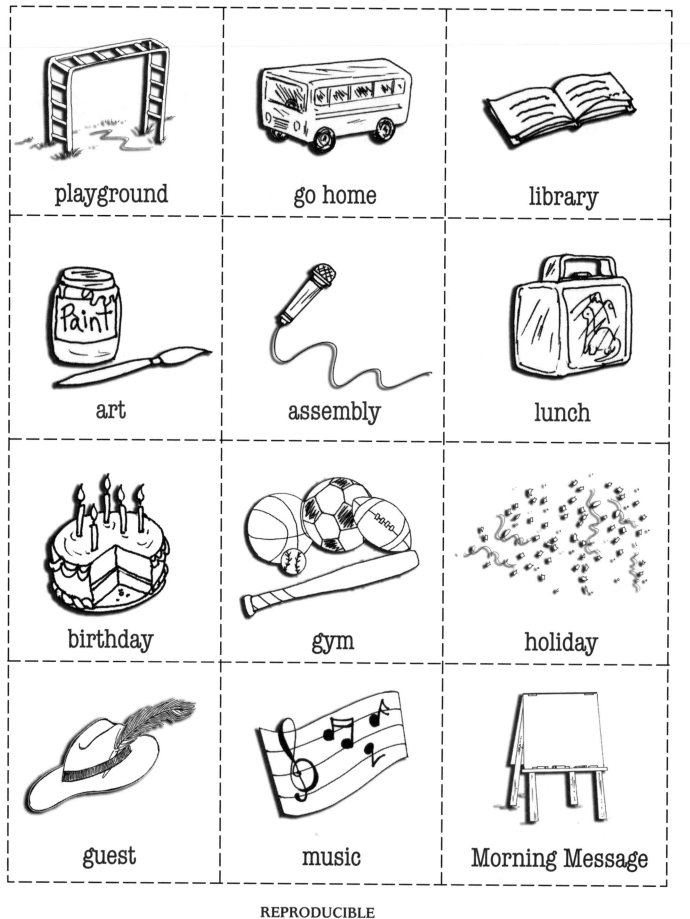

playground

go home

library

art

assembly

lunch

birthday

gym

holiday

guest

music

Morning Message

THE CALENDAR

Graphic organizers are nothing new—we were using them long ago. Anybody who's ever counted to 100 days of school has seen an opportunity to teach math with a graphic organizer. It's called a calendar. If only we'd been smart enough to package it! Now you can actually buy prepackaged programs for teaching math concepts with calendars—and you were already doing it years ago. So bring your calendar into Morning Meeting. In kindergarten, and in first and second grades, calendar time becomes math time. Just use your calendar every morning to teach basic math concepts. There are all kinds of ways you can play off the calendar.

Riddles

You can make up little riddles about today's date. That's one the kids like because they know what the question is going to be. They can get prepared before they come. If today were the ninth, I might say, "I'm looking for a problem that has something to do with 9."

And somebody might say, "Nine plus 0."

"That would be 9. Anybody have a different one?"

"Eight plus 1."

"Eight plus 1 would be 9."

There are lots of different ways to get to 9. That lets kids level their abilities. It helps you assess what they've learned.

If you ask, "What do you notice about this number?" you know what you're going to get? You're going to get little Courtney, who says, "Nine! That's in my phone number!" Or "That number's on my house!" That's all she knows. And then you're going to get Amanda, who says, "Nine would be 2 times 18 divided by 4." That's where she is. That's okay. It lets everybody bring whatever they know about the number 9. (I know: A lot of these are actually math facts. But it's more fun to call them riddles!)

It's important to give kids those opportunities to play with numbers and to level your teaching to what they know about a particular number—as opposed to what they don't know. That's one way to play off the calendar every day. You're building number sense.

WHAT=9?

8+1

9+0

2X18÷4)

Money Concepts

You can have fun with money combinations on a calendar, too. "Today's the 16th. Can anybody show me that in money? What's 16? Is there more than one way to show it?" Maybe Amanda says, "We could use three nickels and a penny." Put the coins in the little flap on the calendar so that you can see them.

Tomorrow, if I'm Stephen and you ask me, "Can you find a way to make 17?" I know what I'm going to do. The only coin I know is a penny, so I'm going to say, "Use a dime, a nickel, a penny, and add a penny." Because it's one more day. They start to understand that. Make sure you run out of coins, because you slide them in there and it's like a visual for them. And then when you run out of pennies you say, "Well, we don't have any more pennies. I guess we can't do this anymore. Can anybody think what we can do?" Maybe we'll trade some of those pennies for a nickel.

Just make sure you run out of pennies!

Odd and Even

To teach odd and even, alternate colors on the numbers of the calendar. "Can somebody show me an odd number here? An even number? What's my hint? That's right: Can I share with a friend and have the same amount, or will there be leftovers? If there are leftovers, is it an odd number or an even number? That's right: it's an odd number."

I think it's fun to make copies of the cookie patterns on page 75. Start with three "cookies." Ask the children, "If I take one and you take one, do we have any left over? Does that mean that three is an even number or an odd number?" You can repeat this all the way up to 13.

Other Calendar Activities

There are all kinds of other ways you can use calendars to explain basic math concepts. How many of these things are you already teaching with calendars?

Patterning. Show the dates in a pattern of red, purple, red, purple, and so on. Ask, "What color do you think will be next?" Or, with older children, look at the pattern in the numbers themselves. "There's a 7. Right under 7 is the number 14. Why is that? What happens when we add another week? That's right: we add seven days."

Building number sense. Say to the kids, "Show me '9.'" They can stamp their feet nine times. They can tally nine. They can count out nine stickers or draw nine smiley faces. They can write the word *nine*.

Skip counting. "Here's 5 and here's 10 and here's 15. Can anybody show me what comes next?" Point out the patterns as you count by twos or threes or fives.

Geometry. Combine patterning and geometry by marking the dates with geometric shapes. "Oh, the number 1 has a circle on it. The number 10 has a circle on it. But gee, the number 2 has a triangle, and the number 12 has a triangle. I think I see something similar about these numbers on this calendar." Reinforce the concept of shapes.

Morning and nighttime. "We're here in the morning with the calendar. What happens before I see you the next morning? That's right: there's a night."

Time of day. "Do I see you at 2 A.M.?"

Yesterday, today, and tomorrow. "Today is Wednesday. What was yesterday? What day will tomorrow be?" You're pointing out the circular pattern.

Before and after. "Next Monday is the 10th. What comes before the 10th? What comes after it?" You're teaching ordinal numbers too!

Place value. "When we get to the 10th number, we have a ones place (the 0) and a tens place (the 1). That's the 0. That's the 1." Using that language helps as you practice place value into the hundreds to count to 100 days of school.

Mathematical language. "Today is the 12th. Can somebody show me a number that's greater than 12? Can somebody show me a number that's less than 12?" Look for all the opportunities to use the calendar to teach the concepts of greater and lesser, more and less, bigger and smaller, higher and lower.

Sequencing. "We started school on Monday. What day comes after Monday?" "This is October. What month comes after October?"

Graphing. Keep track of the weather on the calendar each day, then make a graph to show the number of rainy days, the number of snowy days, the number of sunny days. Graph the number of days in each month.

Seasons. "This is October. What season of the year is that? What season comes next? What is my visual clue?" Copy the clue card reproducibles from page 78 and tape them to your calendar to reinforce which season it is.

Holidays. "This is December. Can anybody tell me a special holiday that comes this month?"

12th > 8th

A Quick Tip

At Christmas and Easter, stock up on colored cellophane. Stick pieces of the cellophane on the calendar numbers to highlight skip counting and geometry patterns even more.

INTERACTIVE BULLETIN BOARDS

Another piece of Morning Meeting is to share some kind of little activity that the kids have done independently and brought with them to Morning Meeting. I like to use an interactive bulletin board to get the kids started. I used to make fun of the fact that we hated changing our bulletin board. I thought, what does it really do anyway? It's only a decoration. We waste our time. But making the bulletin board interactive really paid off for my coteacher and me. We were able to look at some of our standards, put things on that board that played off those standards, and then work with them in Morning Meeting. Here are some themes that I've found work really well for interactive bulletin boards.

Welcome to Our Neighborhood

"Welcome to Our Neighborhood" is one I like to use at the beginning of the year. For that one, everybody gets a T-shirt cutout, and each kid adds it to the bulletin board. When you're welcoming them to the neighborhood, they have to put things on their shirts that represent themselves.

So if you're a kid in my class, one day you come in and there are magazines on the counter. All you have to do is look through the magazines, find a food that's your favorite, and stick it on your shirt. Or you look through a clothing catalog and cut out an outfit that looks like something you'd wear. Or you cut out a picture from a book catalog to show a book you really like.

Your paper shirt begins to build and tell a story about you, but we don't know whose shirt is whose. You're the only one who knows which shirt is yours. (You know your shirt because it has a number on it, and you know that number. And of course you know what you put on it.) And eventually the kids say, "I saw you put it on the blue shirt," and they start to figure it out. But the whole idea is to play with the board and make it interactive.

Smartieville

Another time we had the "Smartieville" board. (I called my kids my "Smarties," so I called the bulletin board the Smartieville board. If you don't want to use that, you could always use "Jonesville" or "Parkerville" or whatever works with your name. Or let the class make up their own name.) We just stuck up our sign that said *Smartieville*, and underneath we put a concept we'd worked on. We wrote the name of the concept, and we put a picture clue there too. And the kids had to add a picture or writing to the board—something they'd learned about that concept. They didn't have to write it; they could just draw it. So if we said "butterfly," the kids had to draw a picture or write something about the butterfly.

Then in Morning Meeting we'd say, "We noticed a lot of you mentioned the life cycle of a butterfly. What we also noticed is that no one talked about this other part of what we learned about a butterfly." Maybe the essential question of that lesson wasn't the life cycle. Maybe the essential question was "Where do butterflies migrate?" And nobody got that! So it gave us a way to assess and go back.

What Would You Ask?

For Lincoln's birthday in February, we had a board with pennies. We started with a blank board and then we added this giant penny shape. The kids were supposed to write a question that we could ask Abe Lincoln. We stuck a picture of him on the chair and we said, "If Abe Lincoln were our special visitor today, what would we ask him?" The kids wrote things like "Were you mad you weren't on the quarter?" "Did you always wear that big black hat?" It wasn't a social studies lesson—it was a writing activity. And it was just fun. The kids were funny. One wrote, "Did you go to the trial of the guy who shot you?"

This is so adaptable to other people too. You could have questions for a teacher or a child or a favorite storybook character. It's a great way to let kids practice asking questions.

Eggs-traordinary Kids

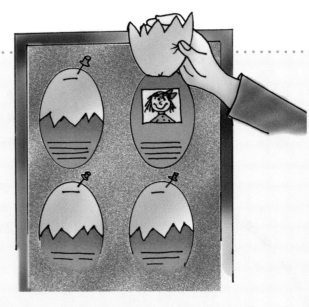

Here's another interactive bulletin board that can be a lot of fun. Make enough copies of the reproducible egg on page 82 so that you have one egg for each child in the class. You see how the top of the egg flips up? Under the top of each egg, we put a digital photo of somebody in the class. We called them our "Eggs-traordinary Kids." We told the kids that each day they were supposed to guess who was in one egg. If they guessed wrong, then they should write a clue on the egg for the next person.

I wrote one clue on each egg. That got things started. So maybe the first day a kid would come in and look at an egg and it would say, "It's a boy." And she'd think, "Is it Carter?" But it wasn't. She'd flip up the lid of the egg and see that it was Matt. So then she'd add another clue. She'd write, "It's a boy who's tall." And the next day somebody else would pick up that egg and think, "Is it Andrew?"

Andrew was tall and he was a boy, but he wasn't the one whose picture was in that egg. So this child would add another clue: "This boy wears glasses." And the next child to pick up that egg would think, "Oh, it's Matt."

If a kid "got it" without adding any more clues, then she could put her initials on the egg on the bulletin board. And then she'd move on to the next egg. The kids could write on a different egg every day. The only one they couldn't write on was their own.

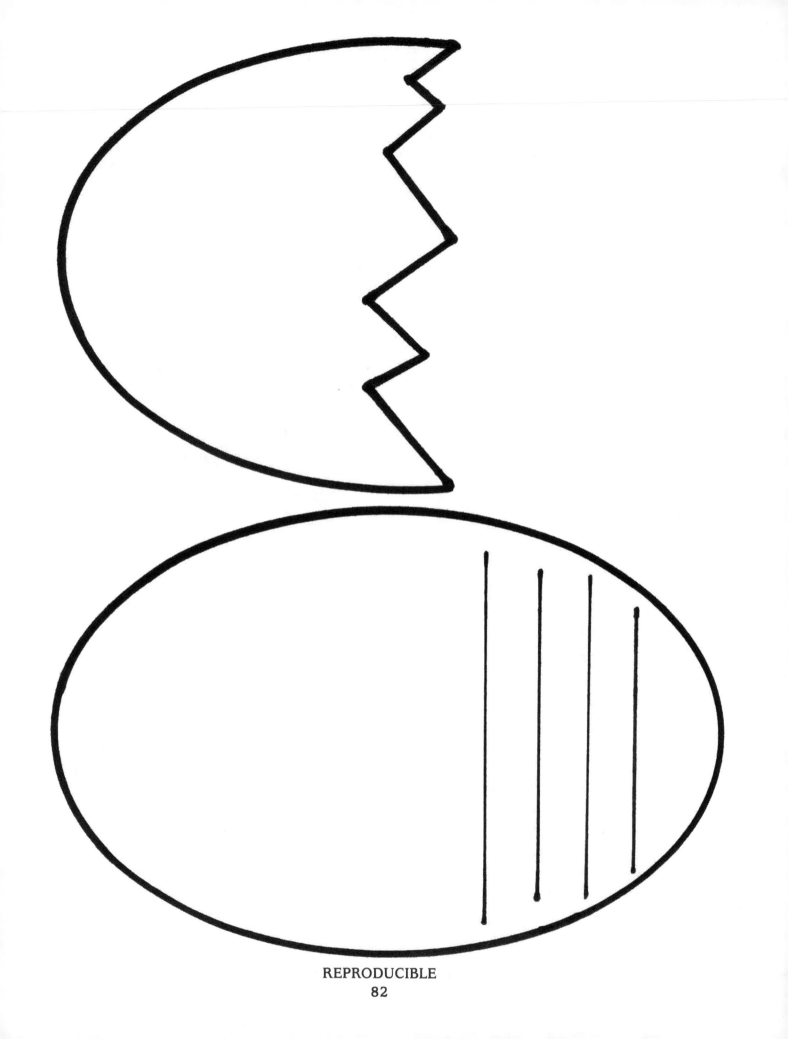

Other Bright Ideas for Interactive Bulletin Boards

I love to use an interactive bulletin board in my class because it's one more thing you can play off with the kids, and because I'm using the classroom environment as a teaching tool. I could go on all day about the possibilities! These are more of my favorites:

Who Would You Like to See "Pop" In? I would put up a picture of a popcorn kernel to give kids a visual clue. Then each kid was supposed to put up a picture of somebody they'd like to see "pop" into the classroom, and write or draw something he would ask that person. It could be the kid's grandma, or it could be Dr. Seuss. If it was Dr. Seuss, the question might be, "Why is the Cat in the Hat's hat so tall?"

We're a Perfect Fit. Take a big piece of colored paper and cut it into jigsaw-puzzle-shaped pieces. Give each child a piece of the puzzle and ask him to take that piece and write or draw his favorite food on it. Then get the kids to put all the pieces back together on the bulletin board.

Smartie Publishing's Newest Titles. Take all the class books your kids have made and punch a hole in the corner of each one. Fasten a book ring or a chicken ring (available from Crystal Springs Books) through that hole, then hang each book from a giant colored tack on the bulletin board.

Tool Board. This is to teach "How can we find out?" You can put up cutouts of screwdrivers, wrenches, and hammers. (If you want, make copies of the reproducibles on page 88.) Tell the kids to fill in the tool outlines with ways they can find things out: They can look in a book. They can go online. They can ask a friend. If they want to know how to spell a word, they can use the environment. That might mean looking at the word wall. If they want to learn about pigs, they can ask a farmer.

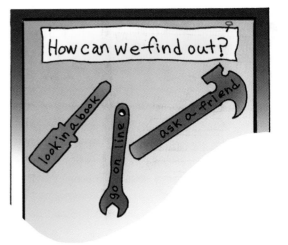

What Lives Here? This is a great way to find out what your kids are interested in. Change the background of the bulletin board to make it appropriate for each habitat. You might put up blue paper and ask, "What Lives in the Ocean?" Then the kids draw pictures of different animals that live in the ocean. You want to pay attention to what they draw. If everybody draws a picture of a shark, then you need to do something with sharks, because clearly that's something that interests them.

Keys to Speaking (or **Keys to Writing** or **Keys to Reading**). Start with the key reproducible on page 89. Enlarge it on the copier, make enough copies for everyone, and then have the kids fill in those patterns. They might say, "Face the person you're talking to" or "Slow down" or "Speak clearly."

Computer News. Set up a computer near the bulletin board. Have the kids go to nbc.com or usatoday.com. Ask each child to print an article that interests him and post it on the bulletin board. Or you can bring in newspapers and have them do the same thing with clippings from those.

Give Me Words. For this one you put up a picture of somebody's face before you start studying something, and later you give the kids a bunch of speech bubbles (see reproducibles on page 138). Each kid is supposed to write in his speech bubble something that person would say. So if I put up a picture of Ben Franklin, then later somebody might write in his speech bubble, "I'm sure glad I kept trying with that kite!" You don't have to use just people. You can put up a picture of a magnet, and a kid might write, "I can't pick up rubber bands." It's a good way to reinforce what they're learning.

Hamburger. "We gobbled it up!" This is kind of like a graphic organizer. You start with the reproducibles on page 87, which show the parts of a hamburger, and stick those on the bulletin board. The topic would be the meat of the hamburger. Maybe that's the weather. Then the other pieces show what the kids have learned. Maybe the lettuce is the water cycle and the cheese represents clouds. The top bun and the bottom bun would be interesting facts. You have to put all the pieces together to understand.

Country. This is a good way to help second graders keep track of what they've learned. Maybe you put up a big outline of Australia, and the kids draw or write on it whatever they know about Australia. Maybe they know what animals live there, or what kind of food people eat in Australia, or what the weather is like. Then, as the month goes on and the class is learning more, you say, "Maybe we ought to put that on our bulletin board because that's something we know now."

 Planet. This works just like the country theme, except you apply it to Mars or Venus or Saturn.

Teacher's Favorite: The Last-Minute Bulletin Board

One of the interactive bulletin boards that I used all the time is so easy for teachers. All you need is a piece of paper with two columns. (See the reproducible on page 90.) Laminate that piece of paper and you can use it over and over again on the interactive bulletin board.

This is great because it's a no-think chart. All you have to do in the morning as a teacher is stick the chart on the board and write the question above it. "Which animal do you like better, duck or horse?" It has to be a question with just two possible answers. And you have a bunch of clothespins. Each clothespin has one kid's name written on both sides. So each kid grabs his clothespin and puts it on a block to show which animal he likes better. And then we play off it as a math activity.

Maybe the question is "Have You Ever Slept in a Tent?" You mark one column "Yes" and one column "No." Have each child put her clothespin on the side that gives her answer. Then you ask, "How many more have slept in a tent than have never slept in a tent?" Of course, first you have to ask, "Has everyone put up a clothespin? How would we know? That's right: we need to count the clothespins."

Questions for the No-Think Chart

It's no-think for the teacher, but the kids still have to think about it! Here are some topics you might try:

- Do you like summer or winter?
- Do you like spring or fall?
- Favorite holiday this month
- Number of people who sleep in your house: 0 to 4, or 5 or more?
- Number of pets: 0 to 3, or 4 or more?
- Letter of first name: Is it in the first half or the second half of the alphabet?
- Favorite number: Is it odd or even?
- Shoe size: Is it less than or more than 2?
- Height: Is it less than or more than _____?
- Favorite choice for class snack: crackers or fruit snacks?

A FINAL WORD ABOUT MORNING MEETING

Morning Meeting is filled with opportunities. Use it to teach and share, but remember that it should always be based on the children and their needs. Being flexible with your goals on any given day will let you gain more teachable moments than you might ever have imagined.

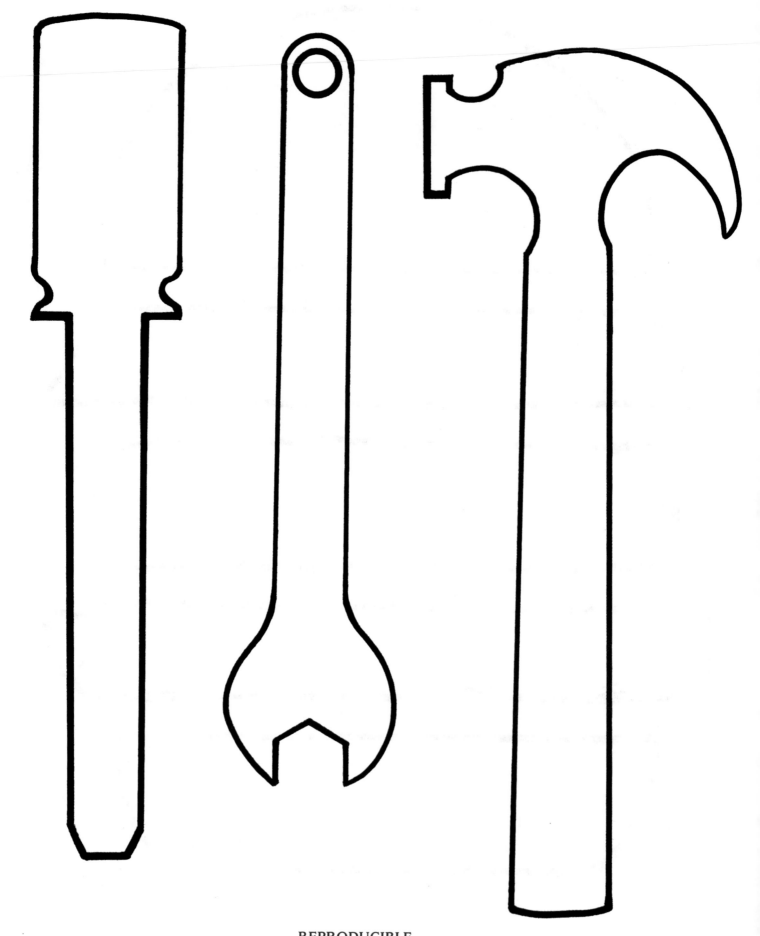

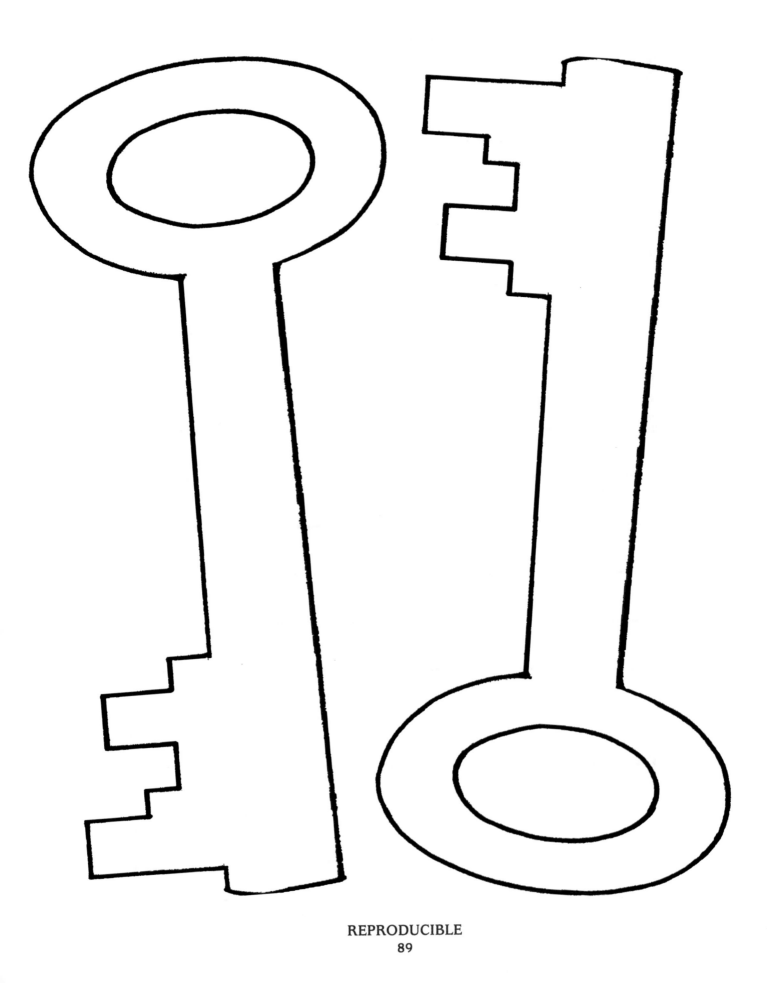

AFTERNOON WRAP-UP

WHAT'S DIFFERENT ABOUT AFTERNOON WRAP-UP

No matter how you structure your Morning Meeting, you want to finish it up in the afternoon. I was a student teacher for a kindergarten one year, and I can remember my first day. I remember how excited I was. And the teacher took out the plan book, and all the plans were written so neatly. It said, "On Monday we will do page 100. On Tuesday we will do page 101. On Wednesday we will do page 102...." And it continued that way, with page 103 on Thursday and 104 on Friday, and so on. Who was going to figure out whether the kids ever got page 101 before we took them to the next step? When were we going to do that? When we tested them two weeks later on the chapter? That doesn't work. Some of these kids aren't getting what we're doing on Monday, and we're pushing them on to Tuesday. Then we say, "Gee, you know what? They're really falling behind." We *left* them behind. We left them back there because we didn't know.

Afternoon Wrap-Up is going to give me a chance to evaluate the day. I'm going to be asking the kids questions. We're going to be working together on some review activities. I'll find out what they got and what they didn't get so that I know what I need to do tomorrow.

And the biggest thing for me as a teacher is that those kids aren't going to go home and do what my kids did to me as a parent. You know what that is: When I said, "Hey, what did you do in school today?" And they said what lots of kids say. They said—you guessed it—"Nothing."

We hear that way too much. We don't want kids who say, "Nothing." We want kids who say, "I did this."

I used to say to kids, "Okay, what's the one thing no one in this class is going to say when they get home today and Mom or Dad says, 'What did you do in school today?'"

They said, "Nothing!"

I said, "That's right. That's against the law. That word is not in our vocabulary. It's not acceptable to say, 'Nothing.' You didn't do nothing. If you did, we made a big mistake." Hey, we did lots!

So in Afternoon Wrap-Up, you're going to be giving kids an opportunity to play some review games and discuss their day so that when they go home and their parents ask what they did, nobody will say, "Nothing." And at the same time, you're going to find out what "stuck" for them.

What's Included in Afternoon Wrap-Up

✔ Distributing mail and the home/school folders
✔ "The ABCs of My Day"
✔ Checklists
✔ "I Need to Remember" notes
✔ Story
✔ Getting ready for the Desk Fairy
✔ Review
✔ Looking forward
✔ Closing

Putting an End to the "Nothing" Answer

We all know how frustrating it is: You took extra time to prepare. You spent the whole day working hard with the kids. They were excited. They were learning. And at the end of the day, when the parents say, "And what did you do in school today?" those kids will say, "Nothing"!

We need to change that!

First of all, just the way we question kids stops them from answering the question. "What did you do in school today?" is too overwhelming to a little kid. We need to change the way we ask that. Instead, go straight to what I call the "Information Highway for Kids." Start with the five senses. Ask, "What did your eyes see in school today?" Can they say, "Nothing"? Not unless they had their eyes closed all day. They must have seen *something*. "Did you see the teacher? Any friends?"

"What did you hear at school today?" "Did you hear a new book? Learn a new song?"

"Where did your feet take you at school today?" "What did your hands do at school today?" Start asking them specific questions about their senses, and all of a sudden it's easier for them to recall that information and give it back to someone.

You're building associative memory for kids. We depend on rote memory way too much in our classrooms: "If I just keep saying it, I bet they'll memorize it." We need to build associative memory that leaves the kids saying, "Gee, when she asks, 'What did my hands do?' what I need to do is look at my hands and think about what it is that my hands did and then I'll be able to come up with something." We want to build associative memory in our classrooms.

Purposes of Afternoon Wrap-Up

You can use Afternoon Wrap-Up in lots of different ways to accomplish lots of different things. You need to decide what your goals are for Afternoon Wrap-Up; then you can figure out which activities will get you there. For example, here are some of the things I wanted to cover in Afternoon Wrap-Up in my classroom:

Overview/review. Are you going to do an overview of the day, because you think it's important to bring all the pieces together? Or are you going to review? Those are two options during Afternoon Wrap-Up. I hear from teachers, "I like to kind of outline it." Some people think it's really important to connect the dots for kids: "During math today we learned about graphing. In science we kept track of temperatures. Let's bring those skills together." That's the person who needs to do the overview. I like a review—from the kids' perspective, not from mine. (I'll get to that in a minute.) Maybe you do an overview one day and a review the next.

Figuring out what worked and what didn't. The overview/review gives you the opportunity to do this. That lesson didn't work if nobody's bringing it up. It didn't work if they answer in a way that has nothing to do with the topic. And if they remember the lesson but think it was about something else entirely? You'd better find another way to teach that lesson tomorrow!

Finding out what interests the kids. During Afternoon Wrap-Up, I like to ask the kids what they think we're going to do the next day. One day we read *If You Give a Pig a Pancake,* and I asked them what they thought we'd do the next day. Of course they all said, "Make pancakes!" Afternoon Wrap-Up gives you an opportunity to listen to what the kids say and then extend the lesson in that direction if you can. Sometimes you can't, but boy, those few times that you can might make all the difference.

Returning to the essential questions of the day. I think Afternoon Wrap-Up gives you a better understanding of how well your essential questions were met. At the end of the day we shouldn't say, "What a great day!" We should be able to say, "You know, there was an essential question to that lesson. Did they get it?" Maybe the essential question was that children can identify the life cycle of a monarch butterfly. Maybe you get to the end of the day and you're doing your review, and the lesson on butterflies comes up. If the kids can show that they understand that cycle and can answer questions about it, then they've got the essential question. If they thought the lesson was all about butterfly migration, then they didn't get it. You need to know whether they got it or not. That's what standards-driven education demands that we reflect on.

Evaluating the day. Afternoon Wrap-Up gives me a chance to see how each kid would evaluate the day. That means I want that child to review what he learned today. And I also want him to review his own actions and attitude.

Looking forward. I want to give the kids a chance to anticipate what we're going to do tomorrow and how it ties in to what we learned today. I want them to learn about setting goals.

Having a closing for the day. Having a closing builds in a routine for the end of the day. It makes everybody feel like part of the community. And it's nowhere near as stressful as the "Oh-no-the-buses-are-here" alternative!

Why My Kids Were Packed Up by 3

You can't just wait for the bell to ring and then say they have to leave in five minutes. It takes one child fifteen minutes to get organized and it takes another child two. Jonathan may be all packed up and waiting at the door, and here's Chelsea still looking for her lunch box. But what you *can* do is organize the end of the day so that the kids understand that you can be packed and ready to go home without learning time being over.

The buses arrived at my school at 3:30. I wrapped up my class at 3, because there was a lot to do in the review time, and I wanted to be able to use that as teaching time.

Why Do the Overview/Review?

The overview/review gives you a chance to figure out how best to continue with lessons. Not that you're not going to do page 102; if that's what's in your lessons, you're going to do it. But the overview/review will give you time to say, "What do I have to do to get ready to teach that next page, if they didn't get all of this the day before?" It gives you a better understanding of the children's point of view of what they did. Sometimes that ain't pretty!

I remember one time I had this great lesson in fractions. I'd made my husband cut a wooden circle into eight pieces, and I'd painted all of the pieces in different colors. This was an awesome fractions lesson. I gave the kids these colored pieces so that we could study fractions, and I thought this was great.

Then we got to the end of the day and Afternoon Wrap-Up. I remember I was at my desk, and my coteacher was running the wrap-up. She said, "I'm wondering whether anyone can think of anything we did in math today that you might want to tell your mom or dad about at home." And I was thinking, "Yeah! Mr. Whyte and I spent all that time on this!"

One little girl spoke up and said, "Math? We didn't do math today."

And the coteacher said, "I think we did. Does anyone remember?"

One of the other kids said, "You know, those wooden pieces."

And the little girl said, "Oh! I thought that was about learning to share the pieces."

You know what? I needed to know that. I needed to know that she hadn't even understood that we were supposed to be playing with those to learn about fractions. I'd spent too much of the lesson talking about how to share the pieces. That was important feedback that I needed to know as a teacher. She'd missed the big question! And she'd missed it because she'd focused on something that I'd put too much emphasis on.

So you're looking for their point of view. You're trying to find out "What is your point of view of what I taught today?"

Beginning the End of the Day

We pack up the home/school folders at the end of the day, so when you get your folder back and I tell you to pick up your mail and put it in your folder, that's your warning. You know that you need to get organized and packed up, because we're going to Afternoon Wrap-Up next.

What we *don't* do at the end of the day is pass out papers. Teachers no longer take part of the day to pass out papers. We say, "They're in the mailbox. Pick up your mail!"

"The mail" means any papers that have been corrected, any printed announcements from the office, maybe a book order—any papers or other things that need to go home. All that stuff goes in the mailboxes. You or the student teacher can sort it whenever you want; it doesn't have to take time away from teaching. And if everybody's getting a copy of the same thing, someone just stands at the mailboxes and puts one slip of paper in every mailbox.

Sometimes when they lose something, kids will come and say, "Well, did you find it?" And I say, "Better look in your mailbox, because if I found it, that's where I put it."

A Quick Tip

Mailboxes don't have to be fancy. You can make them by washing out a bunch of old half-gallon milk cartons and stapling them together.

BACK TO THE HOME/ SCHOOL FOLDERS

While the kids are checking their mailboxes, the student teacher is leaving the home/school folders on the kids' desks. Even in kindergarten the student teacher can do this. The kids learn to read one another's names really quickly because we do so many name games. But at the beginning of the year when they can't read one another's names, there's a photo on the little name tag on each folder. Even if you don't know it says *Connor*, you know that's a picture of Connor. All you have to do is look around the room and see where he is.

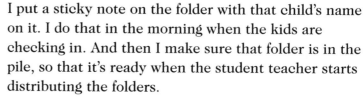

If a student has forgotten his home/school folder and I'm letting him borrow one of the "Mrs. Whyte" folders (see page 36), I put a sticky note on the folder with that child's name on it. I do that in the morning when the kids are checking in. And then I make sure that folder is in the pile, so that it's ready when the student teacher starts distributing the folders.

The student teacher has one other job at this point: while she's handing out the home/school folders, she's also passing out a cup of highlighters, one for every five or so students to share. They're going to need the highlighters for what comes next.

The ABCs of My Day

When you come out of school and start to teach, you're led to believe that if there's a behavior problem, you say to the child, "I'll call your parents." So, okay, you call the parents. And of course the parents are in total agreement with you on everything the child has done wrong, and then the child is so afraid of the repercussions that he is just a lovely child who wouldn't ever do anything like that again.

Yeah, right!

I think there must be a better way to point kids in the right direction. That was the thought behind "The ABCs of My Day." It goes on the right-hand side of the home/school folder. That's the

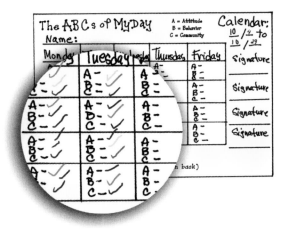

"bring right back" side. "The ABCs of My Day" is the first thing the kids work on when they get their folders back at the end of the day.

"ABC" is shorthand. It stands for "Hey, how was my Attitude today? What about my Behavior? And how did I do as part of the Community?" It's like a behavior log, but it covers more than just behavior. It gives kids a chance to learn what we mean by "attitude" and what we mean by "community." It gives them a chance to practice evaluating their own behavior. And that's a good thing!

On our ABC charts, we used highlighters so that each kid could show how he thought he did that day in each of the three areas: attitude, behavior, and community. We used colors just because when we started it in kindergarten, kids couldn't write letters or words. So we had a definition for each color.

Take a look at the reproducible for "The ABCs of My Day" on page 102, and at the copy of the letter I sent home to parents at the beginning of the year (see page 100). Maybe those will work for you, and you can just make one copy of each for every child in your class. Or maybe your chart or letter will be a little different.

Your definitions may be different from mine. You know what you expect from the kids you're teaching in your classroom this year. You may have different expectations next year. So your definitions may be different, and your colors may be different from the ones we used. That's why there's room on the reproducible for you to fill in your own definitions. But the idea is the same for any class; the difference is just in how you apply it.

In my class, we started by using a green highlighter to mean "super." Blue for my kids meant "good." Yellow was "okay": you had some rough spots today, but you worked on them. We're going to accept that as okay—as a life lesson—and we're going to move on.

(continued on page 101)

A Quick Tip

I used the computer to make labels for the home/school folders. I scanned the kids' pictures in and then I made them little labels that said, "I belong to Connor (or Taylor or Amy or Amanda)." Every label had a child's name on it and his picture. They love labels with their own pictures on them. And that way they can recognize their own folders even before they can read their names.

Dear Parents,

This year priority will be placed on teaching children to solve problems, brainstorm solutions, and evaluate plans. One of the most valuable things we can teach children is to evaluate their attitude, behavior, and teamwork so that they can plan accordingly.

"The ABCs of My Day" will let us work together to help the children reach this goal.

A is for Attitude

B is for Behavior

C is for Community (teamwork)

Each day the children will complete their charts according to how they believe they have performed that day. They will need to use the color coding outlined on the chart. I will be checking the charts daily to determine whether the children's evaluations match my own. At times, the children and I will not agree on a certain evaluation. I may ask a child to reevaluate and make a change but will not insist that the child change it for me. Instead, if the student believes he deserved one color and I believe it should be a different color, I will mark the chart with a "DA" ("don't agree"). If you see that on the front of the chart, you should flip the chart over to view my comments.

We will be completing our charts each day. I ask you to sign your child's chart at the end of each week. If you wish, you may also make comments on the back.

If you have any questions or comments, please feel free to contact me. I look forward to working with you to instill responsibility in the children, to ensure a happy and safe learning environment.

Yours in learning,

Red was "unacceptable": you bit someone, slapped someone, swore, or refused to do something. Red was my pen. Let's say I'm coming around the room while you have your home/school folder out and you're filling out the ABC chart for Monday. And I say, "Amy, look at that. You gave yourself green for behavior. Green. What does green mean, sweetie?" Get them to say it. They have to own it to believe it.

"What does green mean again? That's right: super behavior. Ooh, Amy. I'm thinking of this afternoon when we came out of the cafeteria, hon, and you tripped Jennifer. Do you remember? Jennifer fell. But you know what? Green is super. That is not super behavior."

And Amy says, "But I said, 'Sorry'!" Then I might say that it was okay; it still wasn't super. I might say, "I also really didn't like the way you said, 'Sorry.' You remember the two words that go together? You have to say, 'I'm sorry,' and you have to really mean it."

If they need to change the chart, they change it just by going over it with the new color. And you can tell what they mean. That's why we made the lightest one yellow. The "okay" was always yellow because I might say, "Well, it was okay, but really, I thought you did a good job about getting back in line. I might give you the blue." When you put blue over yellow, you can tell it's blue over yellow; it doesn't mix to green. If it was any lower than yellow, it was my red pen. Everybody could tell that one, because nobody else had one. There was no red in the cup. I was the only one with the red pen.

If the kids changed the highlighting to yellow, they normally went over it, and if I couldn't tell that it was changed, they'd put a Y at the end of it. If they changed it to green and I couldn't tell, they'd put a G. Some kids would say, "I don't think my mom's going to know that that was really 'good.'"

"Well, put a G next to it."

They really learn pretty quickly what your expectations are. They even justify. You go by the table and you don't even say anything to them, and they say, "I gave myself 'good,' because after it happened . . ." That's fine. I wasn't going to say anything. I think they do learn to evaluate. And you have to touch base with them quickly.

A Quick Tip

The student teacher is allowed to ask for help whenever she needs it. When I need help, I ask for it. Often in the afternoon you'll hear a student teacher say, "Cara or Amanda, can you pass out the cups while I do the folders?" Or a child will give half the folders to her best friend, and the friend helps pass them out.

The ABCs of My Day

Name: _____

Calendar:
__/__ to
__/__

A = Attitude
B = Behavior
C = Community

Monday	Tuesday	Wednesday	Thursday	Friday
A - B - C -	A - B - C -	A - B - C -	A - B - C -	A - B - C -
				Signature _____
A - B - C -	A - B - C -	A - B - C -	A - B - C -	A - B - C -
				Signature _____
A - B - C -	A - B - C -	A - B - C -	A - B - C -	A - B - C -
				Signature _____
A - B - C -	A - B - C -	A - B - C -	A - B - C -	A - B - C -
				Signature _____

Green=   Blue=   Yellow=

Red=Unacceptable (check note on back)

But what if Amy wasn't going to change it? She still thought her behavior was super. Was I going to let her take it home and let her parent think she'd been super? No. I bent down and marked it "DA" with my red pen. "DA" next to the child's highlighting meant "don't agree." The parent would flip the page over and see my writing: "I don't agree with her assessment, but she's not willing to change it."

And if you're my student, it's okay if you don't want to change the way you marked something. I can't make you change it if you don't believe it, because then all I've done is control you. You don't really believe it; you changed it because I told you to. So if you're not going to change it, if you really think that your behavior was excellent, then I want you to leave it. But in my eyes that wasn't super behavior. It's something we need to work on together over the year. And your parents need to know that.

There's another side to looking over what the kids have marked, and that's our Alenas and our Erins, who don't realize how golden they are. These are the classic kids who get passed over because they demand nothing. No matter what you ask them to do, they try to do it to the best of their abilities. And then I'd get to the end of the day and I'd see Erin giving herself yellow. I'd say, "Erin, honey, what does yellow mean on attitude?" She'd say, "Okay." And I'd say, "Okay?! Erin, I wish I had 22 of you, sweetie!" We need to remind them. So I'd write "DA" on her chart as well. And then I'd flip it over and write, "I think Erin had a super attitude today. She did this," pointing out to her what she did that made it super.

Ashley hit Nicole today. Now I'm looking at Ashley's ABC chart at the end of the day, and she's given herself green for super behavior. So I say to her, "Ashley, was that super behavior?"

And she says, "I know. Maybe it's not super. But I did say 'I'm sorry.'"

"Do you think that's good, Ashley?"

"Yes."

Well, I can agree with that. I can live with that. I can't live with "it's super," but I can live with "it's good" because I did like the fact that she apologized. If she'll change it to "good," then I'm going to scoot on to the next child.

But if she refuses to change it, I'm going to say, "Okay, but I need to let your mom and dad know that Mrs. Whyte doesn't agree." She can feel that way. She has the right to do that. But the truth is that I don't agree. And so I'll put a red "DA" next to her green highlighting. Then I'll flip the chart over. On the back I'll write, "There was a hitting incident. Ask Ashley."

Watch Your Language

With little kids, it's all in the language. Never use angry words. Kids react so differently to you when you don't sound mad. And don't look mad. Your manner means a lot. Explain that a child has made a bad choice and there are consequences for that choice, but do it in a matter-of-fact way.

I'll use Corey as an example because he was the extreme. He would crawl under the desk. When it was time to start something new, he'd climb under the desk and start kicking and screaming. He didn't transition well. That was the bottom line: he didn't transition well. Then I had two choices. I could say, "Corey, get out from underneath that desk and get in this line!" And I can tell you, nine out of ten times, if I got within distance, he was going to spit at me. Because that's what he did: whenever anyone made him mad, he spit. My other choice was that I could keep my face from looking mad and say, "Corey, that's not a good choice, hon."

The bottom line was, he'd already made it. Get over that part and figure out how you're going to get a kid like Corey somewhere else: "You made a bad choice, babe. Right now you have two choices. You can get out from underneath the desk yourself and get in line, or you can take my hand and I'll take you over there. But this is not a choice that's acceptable, so which choice do you want?"

I gave him back his power. The minute I started doing that, nine out of ten times, he was out from under the desk and in line. Wasn't that what I wanted? There would still be that one-in-ten time when I had to physically remove him and carry him down the hall while he was spitting at me. I admit it! But one time in ten was better than every time!

I didn't even realize it until someone pointed it out to me, but I use "babe," or "sweetie," or "hon" a lot. It softens the message, so I can say, "That was a bad choice, hon," without sounding mad at the child.

We tell the kids to "use kind words." We need to remember to do the same thing. In the end, no matter what, the whole class is built on "good choice/bad choice."

The red pen is the most serious one, and you have to be careful using it. I think sometimes teachers get into this "control freak" mode. A teacher might not even realize it, but she starts feeling like "I'm going to control the kids in this class." That's when the red pen becomes the teacher's chance to pick on everything. That's not good.

You can have control without going overboard. I don't want to control how the child feels about it, but there are times when there has to be a red check on that ABC chart. If there's a red check, Mom and Dad are going to get a phone call from me, or a note home that they need to sign.

The red check is more serious than a "DA." It's more than just "Read my comment about the tripping." It's for something that's totally unacceptable. I need a note back, or the parents will get a phone call from me tonight about what happened.

I'll just walk by and mark that red check on the chart. It's often to save time. If you're my student, I don't have time right now to explain to you why I feel that your behavior was so serious. We probably already talked about it when it happened, when you poked James in the eye. But the truth is that I need to talk to your mom and dad about that because James had to leave the room and go to the nurse, and I told you what I'd do. I'm going to give your mom and dad a call later. I don't have time at the end of the day to go through that with the child, but I try to mark the red check on the ABC chart so that the child knows I'll be in touch with the parents about that behavior.

A red check doesn't have to be for behavior. A child can get a red check for attitude or community, too. Maybe I said to Matthew, "I really need you to try to sound that out," and he said, "No!"

I said, "I really need you to work on your morning work."

"No!"

"I need you to join the group."

"No!"

Matthew refused all day long. He wasn't willing to try. That gets a red check.

A Quick Tip

You don't always have to use the same colors on the ABC charts. Change the colors once in a while, just to keep it interesting.

What If You Lose Your ABC Chart?

I want the kids to know that it's really important for them to fill out their ABC charts and for me to end up with them at the end of the month. If a first or second grader loses his ABC chart, I tell him I don't have any more copies. I don't make any more copies than I need for the month. So I tell kids, "If you lose yours, you have to put a blank paper over someone else's chart and trace the chart." I say, "Well, if I lost something that somebody had written to me, I'd have to rewrite it." They don't like tracing those charts—so they really try not to lose them!

In kindergarten, if you lose your ABC chart, then your job is to ask for another copy, put it into your folder, and bring it to the teacher, so the teacher knows why you're starting your ABC chart on the 15th of the month and not on the 1st.

I'd use a red check for community if a child said, "I didn't read any books today. I'm not cleaning up the book center." It's when a child point-blank refuses to be a part of our class community. That transfers to the playground, too. You're wasting the class's time if you're not in line for recess, because that means we're all waiting for you, and nobody gets to go out to the playground until you're ready. And the other kids aren't going to be very happy about that! So that gets a red check. The red check is for something that goes beyond a few reminders. It's for something serious enough to "write home about."

Of course, if you want to change a child's behavior (or attitude or sense of community), you need to do more than just put a red check on the ABC chart. Kids aren't willing to change if they don't see anything wrong with what they do now. Often you'll have a child who says, "I don't have a problem with my attitude!" He doesn't? Kids need to see a model of what's appropriate, and they need to see it in a less threatening situation. When a child is talking to you that way, that's not the time to model it because he won't get it. But if you model it and point it out during Afternoon Wrap-Up each day, you can make the point.

"You know, I watched Erin today. What a great attitude she had. You know what I liked about it?" You point out what's good. You also give kids an example of what a bad attitude is. But you have to show them what's bad about it when it's not happening.

I'm big on "no whining." Whining does not solve problems. There's a time at the beginning of the year when I brainstorm with the kids what some of our choices are when we have problems. And I'll say to them, "Okay, I think I'll add this to the list. One of my choices is 'I'll just whine about it.' Want to see me whine?" You do it the way they would—but before they do it. And you say, "Now is that going to solve Mrs. Whyte's problem? Does anybody have a better idea today?" You want to have them look at it and start to evaluate it.

Another time, I might model how they could handle the problem. They all knew I was always losing my coffee cup. So I'd say, "Uh-oh, Mrs. Whyte's lost her cup again. Now what am I going to do? I know that whining won't help me find my cup. What else could I do? Maybe I could ask a friend whether she's seen my cup. Erica, have you seen my cup?" You have to show them that there's a better option.

Long-term change requires a child to look at what he's doing now and see something wrong in it himself.

Each ABC chart lasts for a month. Parents sign it at the end of each week. At the end of the month, I file each ABC chart in the individual folder I keep for that student. I use those charts to track the kids' progress during the year.

A Report Card for the Teacher

Every day, you're going to ask kids to evaluate themselves and then you're going to review what they say. While you're doing that, I think it's fun every once in a while to let the kids evaluate you. So the reproducible on page 109 is a report card for the teacher. Every once in a while we bring it out at Afternoon Wrap-Up, and I say to the kids, "I'm going to need your help. You're going to decide what kind of teacher Mrs. Whyte has been today." They know the choices are "always," "most of the time," "sometimes," "never," and "don't know."

So I'll ask, "Was I kind today? What does it mean to be kind?" And we go through it.

I want to share with you a sample teacher report card that two little girls did for me during recess one day. This was a second-grade classroom. They brought it to me and they said, "We did your report card." They had picked up the form from the Afternoon Wrap-Up area.

The first line was "is kind." And I got an A plus, so I was feeling good about that. But on "is fair," I'd been demoted to a lowercase "a," and I was wondering what that meant exactly.

On "listens," I was having a little problem there. I got a B. So that meant that most of the time I listened, but some of the time I wasn't listening to them.

The next line said, "is humorous." They'd asked me what that meant, and I'd said it meant to be funny. I got an A there. They probably did think I was pretty funny that day because that was the day I'd shown up at school with one black shoe and one navy one. They thought that was pretty funny.

After that was "expects the best." I liked this one because they wrote an A, and then somebody took the time to trace it. So I thought that was pretty good, and it was important for me to know that.

Then I got to the next line: "is organized." Not only did I get a D, but I got the lowercase "d" that goes with it! That was pretty bad. So I was thinking, "The kids see that in me. They notice that often I'm running around saying, 'Has anybody seen my coffee cup? I don't know what I did with that paper! Have you seen that paper?'" It reminded me that kids see not only what happens but also how the teacher reacts to what happens. I think of that, and it often reminds me to slow down with the kids.

The next line was "has a clean desk." I got a D minus! But I got an A for "is understanding." And probably the reason I've kept that report card all these years is that they said I was fun. And to me, that's the most important thing I can do in my classroom: make sure they know that learning is fun.

Report Card for: _____

| A=Always | B=Most of the Time | C=Sometimes |
| D=Never | ?=Don't Know | |

My teacher . . .	Rating
is kind.	
is fair.	
listens.	
is humorous.	
expects the best.	
is organized.	
has a clean desk.	
is understanding.	
is fun!	

Sometimes it's really hard to change a child's behavior because he doesn't see anything wrong with it. A kid may think that when you're mad, what you do is hit the person who made you mad. He thinks that fixes it. Getting kids to understand that it doesn't, and to be able to say what would have been a more appropriate response, is something we should be modeling.

"You know, you guys have made me mad today. Mrs. Whyte is feeling really angry." Maybe they didn't behave in the cafeteria. We've all had that. We get there and the cafeteria lady says, "You have the worst class in the building!" That makes you feel just great, right? So you get them in line and get them back to the classroom. You're mad. You know they know the rules; they don't choose to follow them. You talked to them about it just yesterday.

That's when I say to the kids, "I'm disappointed. In fact, I think I'm even a little hurt because you guys know the rules and you choose not to follow them. In fact, I think you guys better give me a minute." And I put my hand up to my eyes and I turn away from them. You do that and they all look so sheepish. We need to model this: What do I do when I'm mad? Do I go around and slap each one of you? That's not an option. That's not a choice.

The idea is to get them to look at these things.

Everyday Checklists

In your classroom, let's say you always send a book home with each child. How are you going to make sure that book goes home? Are you going to accept the excuse the next day that "I forgot my book"? Or are you going to take preventative measures? Are you going to give the kids a way to remember the book every day? If the book is part of what's supposed to go home every day, then when you get your home/school folder back at the end of the day, one of the first things you should see there is your checklist. And one of the first things you should see on that checklist is the book. Getting kids used to that organizational habit, so that they can't use the "I forgot" excuse, is really important. There's a reproducible for an everyday checklist on page 114; I'd recommend that you add whatever is appropriate for your class, and then make lots of copies.

In my class, I had some of the kids check: Do you have your mail? Do you have your homework? If you're taking home your book, do you have it? Do you have your ABC chart in your folder?

And then the last line on the everyday checklist was for "A Good Answer." For what? For when Mom or Dad asked, "What did you do at school today?" I always said, "You won't be able to check that one yet!" And then we'd go to Afternoon Wrap-Up, and part of Afternoon Wrap-Up was finding a good answer. But I loved it when the kids got to the point where they said, "I'm going to check it now because I already have a good answer!" That's the whole point.

We did ruin some folders doing this, but we stapled a whole bunch of checklists—as many as we could get into a book-stapling machine—onto the left pocket of each folder. Each day the kids would go through the list and put a check mark next to each thing they had. The next day we'd pull off the top sheet and they'd do it again, until they were really used to doing it.

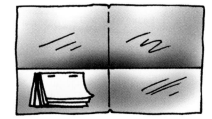

Then we'd make one more checklist for each child. This one we'd laminate and staple to the same spot where the pad of checklists used to be. Then all a child had to do was read through the checklist to be sure he had everything.

We did that unless the child never got it. Sara had a pile all year long. I'd say, "Sara, hon, I want to see actual checkmarks that you did that."

The idea is that the children can go down through the list and ask, "Do I have this?" And they actually check off each thing—making them more responsible and you less of a checker.

You might list other things as well. The checklist is totally individualized for your class. If you expect a book to go home every night, then put a book on the checklist. If you send home homework every night, then put homework on the list.

I didn't use homework every day in my class. We used "fun bags." Not everyone got to take one every day, and so kids looked forward to having a fun bag. It was homework, but they didn't know that. So even though every child didn't take one home every single day, fun bags were on the checklist. If a child wasn't taking home a fun bag that day, then she'd write "N/A" on that line, for "not available."

You can also change the checklist for individual students. Because of Sara's outlandish behavior, for instance, we had a personal journal for her. Her mother wrote in it every day; I wrote in it every day. Not everybody had one of those, but Sara's checklist actually said "journal." And then we'd check off that she had her journal. What goes on that list can be whatever is specific to an individual child or whatever the whole class needs.

The "I Need" Checklist

Not every class needs this, but you may want to add another checklist to the home/school folders. This one would be an "I Need" checklist, and it's mostly for school supplies. We used one of these in my class while we were in a terrible budget crunch. Kids were running out of pencils, erasers, and paper. My coteacher and I were spending a fortune. And the other teachers said to us, "Just make a little checklist. Give them copies of the checklist and have them take it home in their folders." So it actually said, "I need pencils," or "I need paper," or "I need crayons." All those can be on the "I Need" checklist in the folder.

The "I Need to Remember" Note

The checklist is for things that kids need to take home. You, the student, have a checklist every single day, and for the most part it's the same: You have your book, your ABC chart, your mail, "a good answer." And then you have the "I Need" checklist when you need to bring in supplies.

Sometimes you also have an "I Need to Remember" note. Maybe tomorrow we're going to be doing something outside, and you need to bring your mittens. Maybe you need to bring back a signature on the field trip slip. Anything like that goes on an "I Need to Remember" note. (See the reproducible on page 115.)

"Oops" Slips

The kids weren't the only ones in my classroom with checklists. I had a checklist, too. Remember the little fun bags that I gave my kids instead of homework? They had to check those bags out. And in the morning my checklist was right in front of me. I had my desk with my place to put the lunch money and other things. I'd look down my checklist and say, "Oh, by the way, Molly honey, you had the money bag."

"I didn't bring it."

"Oops." That meant that Molly needed an "Oops" slip. An

"Oops" slip meant "Oops, I forgot." I'd give Molly one of those slips and she'd need to write in "money bag." (If a child doesn't know how to write it, she can draw a little picture.) It said (to her mom and dad), "Please help me remember it for next class."

If Molly came to school the next day and said, "I forgot the money bag," that would be Oops #2, and she'd take another "Oops" slip. She'd get one more shot. After Oops #3, I'd call home. I needed that bag back because the next kid on the list was waiting for it.

Take a look at the reproducibles on page 116. You'll see that there are actually two kinds of these slips. One is for something the child forgot to bring in. The other is for something the child forgot to do. Each has a space to write what the child forgot. (It's not always the homework or fun bag.) You'll also see that there's a line for the teacher's signature and a line for the student's signature. We've made a deal. You, the student, didn't do what you needed to do, or you didn't bring the field trip slip that you were supposed to remember. You need to bring it by Thursday.

These slips are quick forms to use so that you don't have to write lots of little notes. You can just fill slips out for things that happen every single day. Then send them home in the folders.

Y ou can find lots of teaching opportunities even in something simple like the "I Need to Remember" form. Maybe sometimes you'll go to Afternoon Wrap-Up with your whiteboard to write on. You'll give each child the "I Need to Remember" slip of paper and you'll say, "There's something you need to remember for tomorrow that's very important." Maybe it's the mittens. "I'm going to write that word [or phrase] up there and I need you to put it on your 'I Need to Remember' note." That's one more opportunity for them to learn that word and to practice writing it while you're modeling for them.

Who Needs to Be Managed?

An important part of being a good teacher is that you don't manage kids who don't need to be managed. Eric doesn't need to be managed. Eric goes right down the list without being told. So what if he doesn't mark it? He says, "Do I have my mail? Do I have my homework?" He does it every day! I don't need to manage Eric. He's not forgetting anything. I need to manage the kids who need help learning to manage themselves.

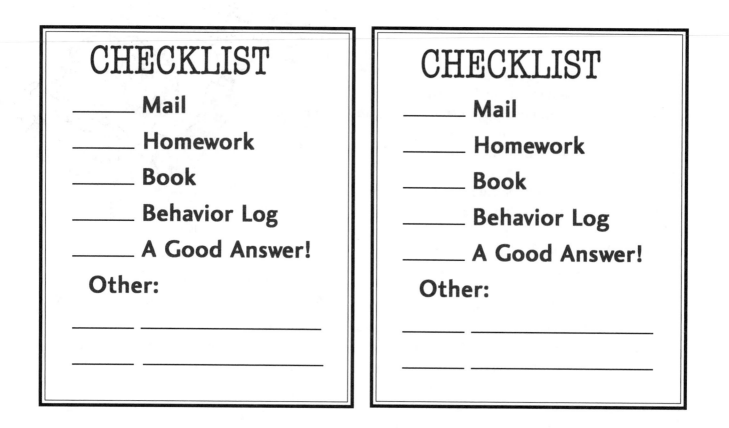

CHECKLIST

_____ Mail

_____ Homework

_____ Book

_____ Behavior Log

_____ A Good Answer!

Other:

_____ _____

_____ _____

CHECKLIST

_____ Mail

_____ Homework

_____ Book

_____ Behavior Log

_____ A Good Answer!

Other:

_____ _____

_____ _____

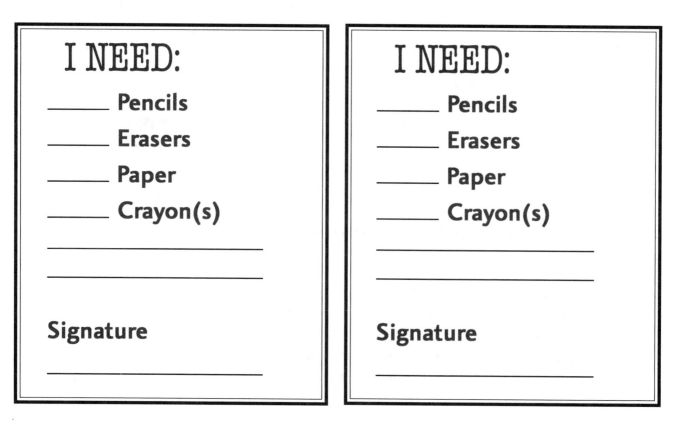

I NEED:

_____ Pencils

_____ Erasers

_____ Paper

_____ Crayon(s)

_____

_____

Signature

_____

I NEED:

_____ Pencils

_____ Erasers

_____ Paper

_____ Crayon(s)

_____

_____

Signature

_____

Name:_____ Date: _____

I need to remember _____

I need to bring _____ by_____

Please help me to remember!

Name:_____ Date: _____

I need to remember _____

I need to bring _____ by_____

Please help me to remember!

Name:_____ Date: _____

I need to remember _____

I need to bring _____ by_____

Please help me to remember!

Name:_____ Date: _____

I need to remember _____

I need to bring _____ by_____

Please help me to remember!

Name _____ Date _____

Oops! I forgot _____.

Please help me remember it for next class!

Slip # _____

_____   _____
Teacher Signature   Student Signature

Name _____ Date _____

Oops! I forgot _____.

Please help me remember it for next class!

Slip # _____

_____   _____
Teacher Signature   Student Signature

Name _____ Date _____

I didn't_____. I need

to _____ by _____.

_____   _____
Teacher Signature   Student Signature

Name _____ Date _____

I didn't_____. I need

to _____ by _____.

_____   _____
Teacher Signature   Student Signature

CHANGING THE PACE
Sharing

Afternoon Wrap-Up began with the kids picking up their mail and packing up their home/school folders. Then we'd go back to our meeting area. I wanted to make sure we ended the day the same way we started it: I wanted to build in that routine, and I wanted to make sure everybody was part of a shared community.

One of the first things you can do in the meeting area is to take a few minutes for sharing. This gives the kids a chance to participate by sharing questions, thoughts, and answers. This is not "Show and Tell." You might take the time to read a poem or two that you or the kids choose. Maybe somebody acts it out, or substitutes some new words in key places. You might sing a song that someone chooses and then leads.

Everybody doesn't necessarily have to share with the whole class. Maybe you have some craft sticks, and you put a number on each stick. The kids draw sticks, and then everyone who has number 2 shares with the other number 2s.

I think it's good to include "Sharing" in Afternoon Wrap-Up. It gives the kids a chance to practice speaking and listening. And that means you're probably going to be able to check off two more things on your state's list of standards.

Book Treasures

Sometimes in Afternoon Wrap-Up you might want to let the kids choose a favorite story to read together again. You know the research: "No activity does more than reading aloud to prepare children for success in school" (Bernice E. Cullinan, *Read to Me: Raising Kids Who Love to Read*, 1992). "Children who come to school ready to read, come from homes where they have been read to" (Marilyn Jager Adams, *Beginning to Read: Thinking and Learning About Print*, 1990). "Reading to children is the most important activity for creating the motivation and background knowledge necessary to read" (Center for the Study of Readers, *Becoming a Nation of Readers: The Report of the Commission on Reading*, 1985).

If it's not happening at home, that experience of reading is something we need to re-create in our classrooms—every day. When a child wants to read, he reads. Generating that spirit of "I can read! I'm motivated!" in kids will make our job easier.

I feel so strongly about this that I wrote a little reader about it called *Read with Your Smartie*. I let the kids know how important it is that we're sharing that activity at home and that it doesn't matter what we read. And I reinforce it by reading with them every chance I get—including during Afternoon Wrap-Up.

The whole premise of reading in the afternoon is to revisit, not to make it something brand-new. We know that rereading old favorites helps create literate children. So for "Book Treasures," you let the kids pick a favorite story.

But how? What if I'm a little kid and you say, "Okay, what's one of your favorite stories?" As an adult, *I* have a hard time recalling that! So we decided that we'd make ourselves some clues. I brought in an old shoe box and we filled it with clues.

I might say after we'd read a book, "Gee, this is a wonderful book. I think this should become one

A Quick Tip

You need to model for the kids what kinds of things make good clues for Book Treasures. If you're going to keep the clues in film containers, then it's going to be important that each clue is small enough to fit in a container. (If you don't use film containers, then you'll probably want to use bigger clues.) Maybe one of your Book Treasures is *I Wish I Were a Butterfly*. Then you can use butterfly confetti. If you read *Mrs. Wishy-Washy*, then you can put a tiny clothespin in the container as a clue. Model a few examples like these and the kids will get the idea.

of our favorites. What do you guys think? If we want it to be a favorite, we can add it to our treasures. What object can we put in the box to remind us of this favorite book?" The class would decide, and whatever they decided would go into the box of clues. If the book was *Corduroy*, they might decide to use a button as a clue. Some of these clues may be tiny. It can be pretty hard to find one little button in the bottom of a shoe box! For me, it was going to be easier to keep track of the clues if we put each one in a film container, so that's what we did. And then we kept all the film containers in a shoe box and all the books themselves—the Book Treasures that the clues reminded us of—in a basket.

So in Afternoon Wrap-Up, we'd bring out the clues for our Book Treasures and we'd pick out a clue. Then I'd say, "This is a story that we've shared before." You can get the kids thinking if you add, "Oh, I can't remember. Someone help me with a clue. What was the cotton ball? Oh, right! It was spilled milk. Let's read our old favorite book, *It Looked Like Spilt Milk*."

The Desk Fairy

Maybe in Afternoon Wrap-Up we're doing "Desk Fairy." The Desk Fairy sometimes checks everybody's desk at night, after everybody's left, to see what kind of shape it's in. I ask the kids, "What's the chance that the Desk Fairy is going to come to my desk tonight?" And I model for them how to deal with that.

The Desk Fairy likes clean, organized desks. She doesn't expect us to be perfect. She expects us to be able to find what we need to do a good job. Are the things that you need to be a good student or the things that I need to be a good teacher in a place where we can find them?

They all look at my desk and shake their heads.

Well then, chances are the Desk Fairy's not coming to see me today.

I let the kids think that the Desk Fairy might come any night, so we always need to be prepared for her. Then every once in a while I model how to get ready for the Desk Fairy. I do that maybe once a month. I say, "What would the Desk Fairy say is an effort to be organized? That's right: The pencils are sharpened. It looks neat." And you know what? I model it and then that night is the night she shows up. What a coincidence!

It's important for the Desk Fairy to notice little things. Some of these kids will never have desks that are totally organized—any more than I will! So the Desk Fairy needs to compliment kids on whatever *is* organized.

In my school, Heather was a little girl who had been in my class a few years earlier. Heather was in seventh grade by this time, and she'd come down and see me after school. So Heather was the Desk Fairy. It was her idea to trick the kids. She'd have a little slip like the reproducible on page 121, and she'd write a little note on it. The kids were always trying to figure out whose handwriting it was.

The note would say, "I visited your desk and I liked it that you had your pencils sharpened before we even started school today." And she'd leave a little pile of silver glitter on that child's desk, so that the kids would think she'd kind of trailed along there. The Desk Fairy didn't hit everybody's desk, but I'd give her some guidance and make sure she got to certain ones.

When kids are young, they love it. By second grade the response is more like "Who put the glitter on my desk?" But it's fun. The only thing is, the janitor may not like it. He cleaned up a lot of glitter in my classroom.

A Quick Tip

It helps if you can recruit an older child to be the Desk Fairy, so that the kids in your class don't recognize the handwriting on the notes. When Heather started as Desk Fairy for my classroom, I modeled for her what I wanted her to do. After that, I made sure she left notes for certain kids, but otherwise she did it all on her own.

Hello!

I visited your desk and I liked it that

Keep up the good work!

Love,
The Desk Fairy

Hello!

I visited your desk and I liked it that

Keep up the good work!

Love,
The Desk Fairy

A Song

You can try all kinds of songs to change the pace and get the kids moving. One example is to get all the kids to sing "If You're Happy and You Know It." Or you can use a song that gets the kids thinking. This is a perfect time to play a CD of a song that teaches them about presidents or the alphabet, and then ask the kids what information the song shares.

Or you can go in a different direction and use the song that originally went, "This is the way we wash our clothes, wash our clothes, wash our clothes." Just change the lyrics to "Joe's [or Jonathan's or Nathan's] going home to his house, to his house, to his house. Joe's going home to his house and this is what he'll say."

Then Joe needs to come up with an answer to what he'll say if Mom or Dad asks, "What did you do in school today?"

GAMES FOR REVIEW & ASSESSMENT

Here's the most important part of Afternoon Wrap-Up: the review. This is when you'll get an assessment from these kids in the afternoon to find out where you're going tomorrow.

How are you going to review the day? You're not going to just sit the kids down and expect them to tell you what went on today. They're going to be sleeping; they're going to be pinching each other. That's when you need some games you can choose from—for overview, review, and looking forward. I have a few games that I use that you might want to put to work in your classroom. The kids think they're fun. I think they're a super way to figure out who got what that day.

- Mum Ball
- Who Wants to Be a Smartie?
- Secret Ballot
- Charades
- That's Bogus
- What If Mom or Dad Asks?
- Hey, What Do You Say?
- A Venn Diagram
- What Adam Missed
- Who Wants to Be the Teacher?
- Guess Crowns
- The Bucket of the Five Senses
- Predicting the Future
- What? Where? How? When? Who? Why?
- I Have/Who Has?
- Beat the Clock

Mum Ball

. . . .

Mum Ball" grew out of the idea that at the end of the day for some quiet time, "mum's the word." The only person who's allowed to talk is the person whose turn it is. Otherwise, if you're in my class and you talk when it's not your turn, you're out of the game. The minute I hear your voice when it's not your turn, you're out of the game.

The kids can sit on the floor or stand, and you throw around the Mum Ball. The Mum Ball doesn't have to be an actual ball. I like to use a Beanie Baby. I used to use a Nerf football that was shaped like a brain, and I loved it, but the kids picked away at it, so I couldn't use that again. The next year I had a mummy doll, which I loved because I'd say, "The mummy is here to play Mum Ball." And the kids liked that, but I couldn't find another one when the mummy got filthy. But I finally decided the best idea is to find a Beanie Baby or some kind of critter with appendages, because it's so much easier for some kids to grab. Many of them can't catch the ball, so that's frustrating in itself, when I need them to concentrate on answering the question. But if the thing you're throwing has something the kids can grab, it's much easier.

What I do is ask a question about the day as I throw the Beanie Baby to a child. I might ask that child something specific—something he did this morning that I noticed. I might say, "Nathan, what did you say when you came to my desk this morning? What did you tell Mrs. Whyte? Tell everybody." And maybe we get to repeat that. Or I might ask a question related to a math or science or reading lesson we've done that day.

But how do you keep everybody else involved? Because Amanda doesn't really care what Nathan told Mrs. Whyte this morning. To keep Amanda involved, sometimes we call "Talk Back" during Mum Ball.

Here's how Talk Back works. I toss the Beanie Baby to Nathan, and I ask him to tell the class what he said to me that morning. So Nathan says, "Now I know the difference between greater than and less than." He had the right answer, so he gets to choose the next child to get the Beanie Baby. He tosses it to Amanda.

Then I say, "Okay, Amanda, talk back. This is the

A Quick Tip

I try to save Mum Ball for a time when I know everyone can have an opportunity. The kids get upset if everyone doesn't get a chance.

only time of the day you can talk back to Mrs. Whyte." "Talk back" means that Amanda is supposed to repeat what Nathan said. The kids like Talk Back. It's part of the game.

The other part of the game goes like this. If the child knows the answer to the question, she gets to throw the Beanie Baby to the next person. If she doesn't know the answer, she throws the Beanie Baby back to the teacher, and the teacher gets to throw it to the next person. If you know it, you throw it. If you don't, you have to throw it back to me and I throw it. Either way you get to throw it, and that's important. It's never good to leave someone out. If you don't know the answer, you still get to throw it, but you don't get to decide who to throw it to.

So then I might say, "Who was listening to what Nathan said?" Somebody will raise a hand. I throw it to that child. He gets to talk back. I say, "You pick. You were on the ball." And then I say, "Boy, Amanda, next time you need to listen, sweetie. Because when we play that game, you want to be able to pick."

So the play-by-play goes something like this:

1. I toss the Beanie Baby to Nathan and ask him a question.
2. He gives the right answer.
3. Nathan gets to toss the Beanie Baby to Amanda, and I ask Amanda to "talk back" by repeating what Nathan said.
4. Amanda wasn't listening to Nathan, so she can't answer. She has to toss the Beanie Baby back to me.
5. I toss the Beanie Baby to Danny and ask him to talk back.
6. Danny was listening, so he repeats Nathan's answer.
7. Danny gets to toss the Beanie Baby to Susan.
8. I ask Susan a new question.

At other times I don't use Talk Back. I just start throwing the Beanie Baby around and asking a question each time it goes out. Once a child has had a turn, he sits on his hands. That way, everyone has an opportunity to participate.

Who Wants to Be a Smartie?

I also play "Who Wants to Be a Smartie?" This started in second grade when the show *Who Wants to Be a Millionaire?* was so popular, and the rules are similar. The kids always were enthralled with that program and they told me they watched it. I thought, "Well, we can play that game. Since I call my kids my 'Smarties,' we'll just change the name to 'Who Wants to Be a Smartie?'"

When we play Who Wants to Be a Smartie? I divide the class into two teams. I ask the first person on Team A a question. Let's say that's Amy. I might say, "Amy, today during Morning Meeting we talked about a different way to write the date. How can you do that?" She might say, "*S-e-p-t.*" I repeat the answer for whoever didn't get it and explain, "That's the abbreviation." I'm hoping this time it sinks in. It might not; that's the reality. But I'm going to keep at it.

If Amy's answer is right, she gets a point for her team, and the next question goes to the first person on the other team. That's Bridget. If Amy is wrong, or if she doesn't have an answer, Bridget gets a chance to answer the same question and "steal the point." Then Bridget gets a new question to answer, so she has a chance to win another point for Team B.

If Bridget doesn't know the answer either, I give the answer and then go back to Team A with a new question.

In this game, you get three lifelines, just like on the TV show—but in this case, it's three lifelines for each *team*, not three per person. The kids love using the lifelines. Each team gets to use each lifeline once. Trust me—within the first three kids they've used the lifelines. I always tell them, "You're not going to have any left for the rest of the game." But they don't care; they use them anyway.

Let's say you're a kid on one of the teams. One lifeline you can get is a "50-50" from the teacher. If I ask you how the date was written in our Morning Message and you don't know, you can say, "Mrs. Whyte, give me a 50-50." I give you two choices for what you might have seen in Morning Message and you pick the right one.

The second lifeline is "Ask the Audience." In this case, it means you can ask the rest of your team—not the whole class, just your team.

The third lifeline is "Phone a Friend." If your class has a play phone, that's the time to bring it out, because the kids love that. I say to them, take your phone and say to the person next to you, "Do you know the answer?" It's that easy.

Sometimes we get other people in the school to play. The principal let us call his office. So our Phone a Friend one day was the principal. If you needed the answer, you could call Mr. Spencer. The problem was, for the questions I was asking, Mr. Spencer might not have known the answers. If he hadn't been in Morning Meeting, how was he going to know?

I told the kids that and they still wanted to call him! They called him up and asked, "How was the date written?" And he said, "Was it 'September'?" And they were groaning. And I said, "Guys! How would he know?" It was a life lesson in itself. Let them use their lifelines any way they want.

A Quick Tip

When you need to divide kids into two teams, you can just split them up according to which side of the room they're sitting in, or you can call off numbers and then have all the odd numbers on one team and all the even numbers on the other team.

Sometimes if they were on the rug, I'd just walk down the middle. I'd say, "If you're on that side you're on one team, and if you're on this side you're on the other team."

Secret Ballot

"Secret Ballot" is a game I made up one day because I was out of time and I needed to write a very important note to send home to a parent. The kids were saying, "What do we do for review?" And I was thinking, "I'm going to write this note to this parent." So I grabbed the recycling box and dumped everything in it out onto the floor, which they thought was funny to begin with. I threw the box down in the middle of the floor and I said, "That is the ballot box. Every one of you, draw me a picture that shows me something you did today and throw it in the ballot box."

I wrote the note while the kids were drawing. Then I picked out a couple of ballots as they were going out the door and I said, "Look at this. Somebody says—what do you guys think this is?"

"That's the butterfly!"

"Ooh, you're right! Somebody says the butterfly came out of its chrysalis today. Did that happen in our class? It's a secret ballot, but that's what somebody says. Who agrees with that?"

They raised their hands. I can still see Andrew, the little guy at the back of the line, shaking his head.

"Andrew, you don't agree with that?"

"No."

"Did you see the butterfly come out today?"

"No."

He'd been in the bathroom. Then he'd gotten called to speech. He'd missed the whole thing. This was my chance to say to myself, "Tomorrow, I need to let him know what went on in our class and at least give him an opportunity to revisit what was an exciting experience for a lot of us."

Secret Ballot was so made up the first time. But later on we made it a regular game. First, each child gets a Secret Ballot slip. That means each kid gets a ballot (see the reproducibles on page 130) with a question or instructions on it. It might say, "What is something we did today?" Or it might ask the child to fill in the blank.

Whatever it says, if your kids are young, in the beginning you'll have to read the slips of paper to them; they won't be reading them because most of them can't read yet. So to answer the question, they draw a picture. Later, for my second-grade class, I actually made up little slips that said, "What is something Mrs. Whyte did today?" "What is something Mrs. Davis did today?" "What is something Matthew did today?" If Mr. Colburn was our guest that day, it might say, "What is something Mr. Colburn said today?" Some of the kids would write, "Hi."

Each child fills out his Secret Ballot and puts it into the box. I don't have time to read or look at all of them. Besides, it's secret! The kids don't know who's going to get picked. They just know I'm going to reach into the box and pull out a couple of ballots. I'm running out of time here! And when I pull each one out, they don't know who put that one in.

The idea of Secret Ballot is just getting kids to recall and giving everyone a turn. I didn't have time—I was out of time. But I could make it kind of fun, and get everyone writing for a minute, while I wrote the note that I needed to send home. And then we played off those slips. And the kids liked it, so that's why I kept it.

Sometimes it's not just the kids who learn from the Secret Ballot game. It can be pretty enlightening to look at all the answers after the kids have gone home. Let's say one day you read a book you just loved to the class. You read *The Lorax*, and you think the kids just loved it too. Then when you do Secret Ballot, you ask the kids what book the class read today. And the answers you get back all say, "We read that l-o-o-o-n-g story!" Then you know you should have spread that book out over several days.

We made birdhouses one time. Every single secret ballot that day said we made a birdhouse. So when I said, "Someone said that we made birdhouses," they were all so proud. And when I said, "Who agrees?" every hand went up! So Tina said, "Look at the slips of paper! They all say we made birdhouses!"

What Do Kids Answer on the Secret Ballot?

The whole idea of Secret Ballot is that it's a very quick review at the end of the day. All you need is one sentence like this one.

Secret Ballot

What is something
_____
said today?

Secret Ballot

What is something _____

_____

did today?

Secret Ballot

What is something _____

_____

said today?

Secret Ballot

Name one thing you know about

_____.

Charades

You can act it out. We do "Charades." Earlier I mentioned two hearing-impaired girls who were in one of my classes. Those two girls taught me more about teaching kids who don't learn auditorily than I ever would have learned otherwise in my whole career. We started playing Charades with them.

We started by saying that no one could talk, so you had to get the information across the best way you knew how. I'd give a child a card that might show the name (or a picture) of a character from a story we'd read that day. Or I'd just tell her to show "The Big Bad Wolf" and she'd have to act that out, until someone could guess it.

It's sad that in America, kids who are four, five, six, seven, or eight don't feel safe being silly. They're embarrassed. It's fun to be silly! It takes time sometimes to get some of them to come out of their shells.

I think of Matthew, the boy who was really gifted. One day his Charade was to show something we'd seen that day. He threw himself on the ground and started rolling around, and I was thinking, "Is he having a fit or is he showing us something?" It turned out that he was showing us how the butterfly had come out of the chrysalis. We were raising monarchs in the classroom during a unit on butterflies. So when Matthew was acting this out, we had to envision the butterfly from the way he was rolling around on the floor and punching out.

I think it's fun to be silly sometimes. You can still review and give them a chance to be silly and be kids.

That's Bogus

This is a game the kids made up. The basic idea is that I'm going to give you several sentences, but only one is true. You have to figure out which ones are bogus and tell me to remove them. I'm trying to trick you, so you have to be on the ball.

I might give the kids these sentences:

We drove to gym.

We ate lobster with melted butter.

We learned to fly.

We used a ruler to measure inches.

It's pretty easy to figure out that "We learned to fly" is bogus. But some of these are harder. I want the kids to look for a sentence that sounds as though it could be true, but there's some piece of it that's not true—therefore we didn't do that today.

"We drove to gym." Hey, we went to gym today. What's wrong with that? We didn't drive there.

"We ate lobster with melted butter." We didn't do that. We ate popcorn with melted butter. So that sentence isn't true.

You keep going, figuring out which sentences to remove, until you have just one sentence left. That's the way the kids see it—and they're right. But in actuality you've also reviewed some concepts that you *did* discuss today by saying what you *didn't* do.

"We used a ruler to measure inches." That was true. We did do that.

In kindergarten, you might start by giving the kids just two sentences, one true and one not. By the time they're in second grade and getting good at it, you might be all the way up to seven sentences.

Narrowing choices is a good skill for children to learn. Kids who play "That's Bogus" now will have an advantage later on, when they need to eliminate some choices on tests before they decide on final answers.

A Quick Tip

If you have time, you can model writing during "That's Bogus," saying the words as you write. Or you can write the sentences on the board before the kids get to the meeting area. Or you can say them out loud. Just about anything is fair game, as long as it will get the kids interested and participating.

What If Mom or Dad Asks?

This was a goofy little chant. It started one day when I said, "If Mom or Dad asks what you did in school today, what are you going to say?" and a little boy said, "I'm just going to say, 'Nothing.'" I said, "If Mom or Dad asks, you'll say, '*Nothing*?'" I don't know what made me think of it, but I started stomping around the room and chanting, "What if Mom or Dad asks? What if Mom or Dad asks?" I was stomping around the room and the kids thought I was being goofy. So I said, "Get up and start chanting." And they got behind me and started stomping and chanting, "What if Mom or Dad asks?" And then I said, "Freeze!"

We did ordinal numbers. I thought, "What an opportunity. I'll say, 'It's the seventh person in line.'" I turned around.

"How do we get to the seventh person?"

"Count!"

"Ooh, good idea! One, two, three, four, five, six, seven. You're the seventh person in line. I have a question for you: What if Mom or Dad asks? What will you say that you did in school today? What's something that your hands did in school?" If they can't remember, this is where your strategies for helping them come in. Kids are put on the spot the same way they are with their parents. So you need a strategy to get them to think it out. How about, "Rachel, can you tell me what book we shared? Or a favorite character in a book today?" Remind her before she goes home.

All my children knew ordinal numbers by the end of the year. It's my belief that the one lesson I taught each year on ordinal numbers isn't the reason. I'm convinced they knew their ordinal numbers because we played this game.

Hey, What Do You Say?

"Hey, Matthew, what do you say? What did you do in school today?" The kids sit in a circle. You start the chant: "Hey, Matthew, what do you say? What did you do in school today?" It's a chant, so you have the kids clap at the same time. You go right around the circle. They're not allowed to repeat an answer. The first answer will be "I ate lunch." The second one will be "I went to gym."

"Okay, guess what, guys? No one else can say 'I ate lunch' or 'I went to gym.' Those are out now. They've already been said."

So you try to get them to talk. The rule is that a child can skip sometimes. She can say, "Skip." At first, sometimes everybody skips. Then it's a pretty short game! If they want to skip, you let them skip. But you really play off the kids who *don't* skip. Some kids have to learn to speak and to interact with the other kids. But once they've learned that, they don't want to skip anymore, because they want to feel that they're part of the game.

Usually on any given day, when someone comes up with a good one, I say, "Oh, when my mother calls and asks me, I know what I'm saying today. I'm saying what Annie said. What a great idea!" They want to be the one who comes up with the great idea that the teacher will tell *her* mother.

What to Do When Things Aren't Going Well

There are some days when I don't hold a wrap-up, because I can see the kids aren't with me. On days like that, are you going to read them a book and end the day quietly? That's what I did. The best way to end the day, if things haven't gone well or exactly as you wanted them to, is with a quiet book.

Often, Afternoon Wrap-Up is that opportunity to say, "We need to play a little evaluation game quickly so that we can figure out what we're going to say when we get home. But then let's share a book that's an old favorite." Revisiting old favorites is a gift that we can give to children.

A Venn Diagram

Maybe you brainstorm. One of the ways I brainstorm with kids is to make graphic organizers. I think some of the best ones are just Venn diagrams. Remember the mental "me" folder that each child is bringing to school with him—the one that says, "It's all about me"? We need to build on that thinking and get them thinking about how the things they've learned tie into their own lives.

So maybe you have a Venn diagram that says to each child, "Here's the character; here's you."

"How are you like the character in the book? How are you like the Big Bad Wolf in the story of 'The Three Little Pigs'? And how are you different?" Maybe you can tie it into what they know already and can play off it.

Maybe you've been studying butterflies. Maybe one side of the Venn diagram is "me" and the other side is butterflies. So if you're a student, you should be thinking, "How am I like a butterfly? Ooh, we both grow. I grow, and butterflies grow." So that goes in the center, where the two circles overlap.

The next question would be "How am I different from a butterfly? Well, butterflies fly around. I don't fly; I walk. So I'll put 'fly' on the 'butterflies' side of the diagram, and I'll put 'walk' on the 'me' side.

What Adam Missed

You might say to the kids, "Adam wasn't in school today, and we had a long day together. Adam missed some things. So we want to put something in his mailbox that will tell him what he missed. We want to recall some important things we did today that Adam missed, so that I don't forget that as a good teacher, I need to go back and talk to Adam about these things. So if you remember something that you learned or did today that Adam might need to know about, I'd like you to raise your hand. Let's write it up here. And then we're going to write who said it." It's funny how the kids don't want anybody to feel bad that they've missed something.

The reproducible on page 138 gives you a bunch of these little quote bubbles. If you expect the kids to fill in the bubbles, you might want to enlarge it when you copy it, so that everyone has plenty of room to write.

The kids like this graphic organizer because everybody has a chance to be included. I like it a lot because it's a great review tool, and because it gives me a way to send home to Adam's folks a list of what we covered. I mark the date on it. That way, if I forget to say something, then at least this went home to his mom, and if she has any questions about it, she can always ask me. It goes into the mailbox of the child who's absent.

In the beginning, you're lucky if the kids fill six of these little quote balloons. It makes me sad—they haven't learned to speak to others. Being able to speak to people is one of the things we're working on. But eventually, the list will get bigger and bigger because everyone in the class wants to add his two cents about what went on.

When you encourage kids to talk, they want to talk. Eventually I made a sheet that had nothing on it except speech bubbles to tell Adam what he missed. We had 18 bubbles. So if a kid wanted to add her two cents, she got to add her two cents. All those cents added up to big learning! We all learned from one another. I'd fill in the speech bubbles as the kids came up with things. Or sometimes we made this the interactive bulletin board. At the end of the day, I'd say, "Fill in your speech bubble and put it on the interactive bulletin board," because we just didn't have time otherwise.

Other Graphic Organizers

Graphic organizers are a great way to review. You can always brainstorm together some ways to fill in a graphic organizer. Just draw a big circle. "Here's today. . . . Give me some things about today." Or sequence it. "What happened at the beginning of our day? What happened in the middle of the day? What happened at the end?" Teach them to use graphic organizers to lay out the progression of things.

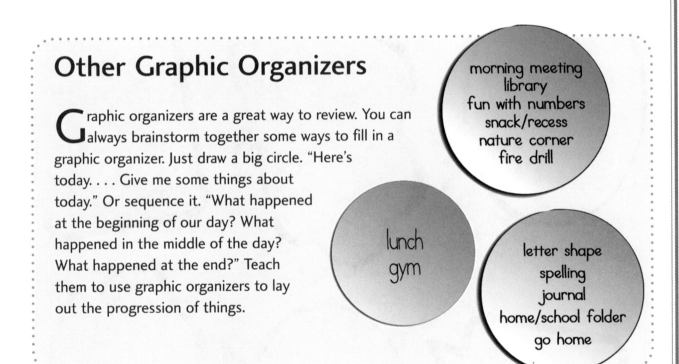

Who Wants to Be the Teacher?

Maybe the class is working on some kind of graphic organizer. You ask, "Who's willing to be the teacher and show Mrs. Whyte doing something today?" Anyone who's ever been a teacher and watched kids play school has said, "I don't sound like that!" They imitate me, and I think it's funny. You should have seen this one kid imitating me searching all over my desk for my coffee cup. It was pretty funny!

They're watching us. We need to be careful to remember that they're modeling how we react to things and what we do, what we say about what we do when we can't write, what we do when we can't read something, what we say when we can't find something. We need to make sure we remember that if we let them be the teacher. It can be a humbling experience!

Guess Crowns

● ● ● ● ● ● ● ● ● ● ● ● ● ● ● ● ● ●

For this one, we make crowns out of manila paper, and then I pick a "Lucky Duck" (see box). And I say, "Okay, you get to wear the crown." So if Alannah is the Lucky Duck, I put the crown on her head.

The key to the game is that if you're the crown wearer, you don't know what's on the crown. You have to ask questions to figure out what it is. If I'm a kindergarten teacher, maybe the first thing I put on every one of those crowns is one letter of the alphabet. So the kids know it's always going to be a letter. When they're older, they can handle a higher level of questions, but I like to keep it pretty simple in the beginning.

The crown wearer can ask another student a question, but the other student can say only "yes" or "no." (If a student gives a wrong answer, then I have to step in and model for that child how to figure it out.) So the crown wearer might say to another student, "Am I K?"

"No."

"Am I *C*? Am I *Z*?"

It's probably better to say, "Am I at the beginning of the alphabet? The middle? The end of the alphabet?" But you have to train them to do that. "Am I between *A* and *E*?"

The crown wearer asks another kid yes or no questions until she gets a "no." Then she moves on to the next child.

With an older kid, you might tell him that what's on the crown has to do with something we learned in school that day. So that child might ask, "Am I a word?"

If he gets a "no," then he might ask the next child, "Am I a picture of something?" Or "Am I a dog?"

I facilitate it by saying, "Guys, remember: Did we see any dogs in our room today? No? What did we do today that might be on that crown?" I'm trying to get them to refocus.

Just the idea that they might have a word is so hard for kids. They need to learn higher-level thinking skills, to take the clues they're getting and put them together. One kid just said it wasn't a word. So then the child with the crown asked whether it was a picture. And then he said, "So am I the word *have*?"

"Well, wait a minute, you can't be the word *have*. We

already established that you're not a word!" Depending on the student's level, sometimes we have to rank things on the board. You need to get them to understand that they can play off the progression.

"Am I red?"

"Yes."

"Am I round?"

"Yes."

"Am I an apple?"

You need to keep them working on the progression so that they can develop higher-level thinking skills.

This builds kids' ability to do riddles, and riddles are a great way to get kids thinking out of the box.

Lucky Ducks

I have two cans, two little "ponds" that we made out of tin. There are sticks in each one. Each stick has a duck sticker at one end and a child's name at the other end. So when I need to pick who goes next, I pick a "Lucky Duck." I go to the first pond and I grab the duck end of a stick and see whose name is on the other end. Once a child has had her turn, I put her Lucky Duck stick in the other pond. All the ducks swim the same way, so everybody gets a turn. And then they all go back the other way.

The Bucket of the Five Senses

We have a "Bucket of the Five Senses." It's a standard beach bucket with cards in it. A child gets the bucket and has to pick one of the cards. (See the reproducibles on page 143.) If she draws a card with ears on it, I ask, "What did your ears hear today?" The child might answer, "I heard Mrs. Whyte read a book." If I want to get her talking more, then the bonus question would be "What was the book?" I don't always use a bonus question, but often I want more. I want to know what the story was about or who one of the characters was. The question mark is "You choose any one of the five senses."

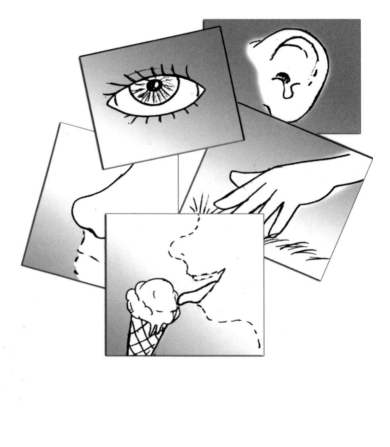

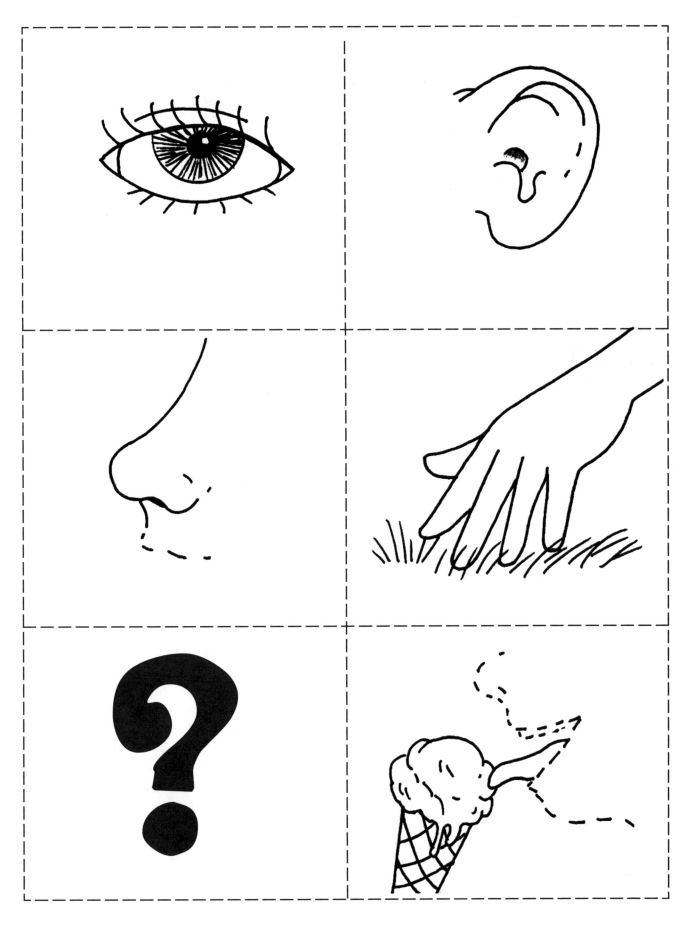

Predicting the Future

Anyone who's ever been a teacher has received some really neat gifts for Christmas and birthdays and the end of the school year. I received a crystal globe one year from a little boy. The globe had a bird inside. Years later, my coteacher and I were eating lunch in our room one day and I found the crystal ball up in the closet. I brought it down and I said, "Hey, do you remember this?" The little boy had left our district; he wasn't around anymore. And I said, "You know, this would almost be prettier if it didn't have the bird in it."

So I got my X-acto knife out of the drawer and I held the thing upside down, and I cut along the globe near the wood. Then I popped off the base and broke the bird off. Then I put the base back on and I said, "Do you think we could hot-glue this and make it into a crystal ball?"

My coteacher said, "Oh, give me a break." But I threw some glitter inside the ball and then I hot-glued it. I put a ton of glue on there so that it wouldn't leak. Of course it still leaked. But I had this "crystal ball" and I remember how enthralled the kids were with it. I'd say, "Today, we're going to look into the crystal ball and we're going to think about what we might do tomorrow. If we learned about the number line today, what might we do with it tomorrow? Let's look into the future." I think one of the nicest things that came out of that was that we did things the kids wanted to do that tied into what they were learning.

We're always predicting for stories and things. Why don't we predict what we might do tomorrow in the classroom? Often the kids will come up with things. One day we were measuring with rulers. And I said we could measure with other things, like strings. So one kid said, "Maybe tomorrow we'll measure with our shoelaces." Kids will come out with things they think are fun. If it's feasible, it's feasible. Sometimes it's not. The kids would predict that we were going to go to the zoo. And I'd have to say, "No, we're not going to go to the zoo." But listening to them is important too. We did measure with their shoelaces. And then that became a lesson in getting all those shoelaces back on their shoes!

One time we were working on dinosaurs, and we looked into the crystal ball. And this little boy said, "I think tomorrow we're going to find some fossils." Uh-oh! But after he left, the other teacher and I said, "Let's go bury some plastic play dinosaurs in the playground sandbox. And then we'll tell them we're going to do what archaeologists do: we're going to go out there and dig for fossils." We had this whole thing going! It was the boy's idea. He was so thrilled! I think it's important to listen to what kids want to know.

We had some problems with the crystal ball. It did leak, for one thing. But what I did instead was make a "future bottle." This one's easy: Put some colored water and a little glitter in a clear plastic soda bottle. Hot-glue the top on, and then shake it. Sometimes I think it's the glitter coming down that focuses kids. Then tell them to look into the bottle and think about what we might do tomorrow. It's not that you're going to see it in the bottle. It's not magic. It's that you're going to think about what we might do with what we learned today.

A Quick Tip

At Afternoon Wrap-Up, I used to take my plan book and put it on the floor and look down at it. If we were playing a game, I sometimes needed a reminder of what we'd done that day. So I'd look down at the plan book and say, "Oh, yeah. Who remembers . . ."

What? Where? How? When? Who? Why?

Start with one slip of paper for each child in the class. On each slip of paper, write either "what," "where," "how," "when," "who," or "why." Put all the slips in an old frosting container, and have a child draw one of the slips. Then the child has to ask a question that starts with the word on the slip of paper he's drawn. So if a child pulls out *why*, for example, he might say, "Why do our teeth fall out?" If the word is *who*, he might say, "Who is wearing black sneakers?" Or if he draws *when*, he might say, "When do we go to recess?" You're teaching kids to ask questions that other people have to answer.

I Have/Who Has?

There's another game I really like for ending the day. It's called "I Have/Who Has?" For this one, make a copy of the reproducibles on page 147. Fill in all the cards, and cut them apart and hand them out to the kids. Then ask the kids to stand up and read their cards in order. The first person to stand up is the one who has the smiley face on the top half of his card. He reads the bottom half. The game goes like this:

First child (reading the bottom of his card): "Who has *A*?"

Second child (reading the top and then the bottom of her card): "I have *A*. Who has *B*?"

Third child (reading the top and then the bottom of his card): "I have *B*. Who has *C*?"

It doesn't take very long to play this game, but it covers a lot of learning. And the real gift of this game is that it's so transferable. You can do letters, numbers, clocks, or shapes. Or you can do geography questions or science questions. It's a great way to do a quick review at the end of the day. You need only one start card and one finish card; you can have as many cards in between as you need.

☺ *Start*	I have	I have
Who has	Who has	Who has
I have	I have	I have
Who has	Who has	Who has
I have	I have	I have
Who has	Who has	*The End!* ☺

Beat the Clock

I don't want for one minute to fool you into thinking that every day everything will be so hunky-dory that time doesn't get away from you. It does. But how you choose to beat the clock makes the difference. You've got to beat the clock. You're running out of time. How can you do it in a fun, lighthearted way that doesn't put kids under that stress of "Get the heck out the door"?

I think you can do it. I think you can set a timer. And you say, "We have to really pick up our feet. Do you know what it means to have fast feet?" That's a little different from "GET GOING!" It makes a huge difference how you choose to end the day and the words you choose to use.

There are going to be times, so be prepared. Don't wait for those times to happen. Know what your strategy is going to be. Are you going to say, "Leave the books. We don't have time to get the books"? Is there ever going to be a time when you realize, "Okay, I'm out of time. If I try to shove this all in, I'm going to stress these kids out and I'm going to stress myself. The mittens are going to be here, the lunch boxes are going to be here. What's the most important thing I need to do to get them out the door in the next 30 seconds? I need their lunch boxes in their hands"?

So: "Everybody make sure you have your lunch boxes, and we're going to need to get going. So don't worry about the rest of it today. We'll worry about it tomorrow." Figure out ahead of time how you're going to handle that. Have you ever played that game "Beat the Clock"? It used a little clock, and that's what I used. It actually was a loud little clock. The kids heard that, and they knew it was counting down, and they'd laugh about it. We did it in a lighthearted way, but the reality is that sometimes that happens. Kids need to get out the door. It's just a question of how you do it. We used that little clock, and when that gave out we used a little one-minute timer that ticked loudly. We wanted kids to hear the ticking the same way we were hearing it.

LEARNING ON THE WAY OUT THE DOOR
The Closing

Would you say to a guest in your house, "Hey, let's go! The car's out there in the driveway!"? Well, we don't want to do that to kids either. We want to say good-bye. We want to see them out the door or out at the bus the way we saw them when they came in.

One way to do that is to play a game that gets the kids to the door. I liked to recite a rhyme that went like this:

One, two, I'll give a clue: It's red [or blue or yellow].

Three, four. When you're at the door [so they have to get to the door in order to play].

Five, six. Who will I pick? [You have to be at the door for me to pick you to figure out my clue.]

Seven, eight. I cannot wait [so if you're not at the door, I'm not going to pick you].

Nine, ten, show me when. [Use our special signal to show me when you're in line and ready with the answer.]

Then I'd pick someone who was in line and ready.

As soon as the children are where they need to be, have them give a signal that shows they're ready. You can have them give a thumbs-up or close their eyes. Or ask them what they'd like the signal to be. They'll come up with some good ones!

You do need to recognize that the kids may not come up with the right answer the first time. You may need to give a second and/or a third clue and say the rhyme again.

Learning Line-Up

When it's time to line up, you can get all hyper. But what's better is to ring a little chime or sing a little song or do a little chant. You might sing a song that's on my CD *Sing Yourself Smart*. The tune is "Twinkle, Twinkle, Little Star," but I changed the lyrics. Try something like this:

Mrs. Whyte's hourglass.
Time to clean up in our class.
Hurry, hurry, don't delay.
Time to put your things away.
Mrs. Whyte's hourglass.
Time to clean up in our class.

Or, to the same tune, sing:

Good-bye, good-bye, my smarties,
Time to go. . . . Line up, please!
Check for notes, books, and backpacks,
Won't be long till we'll be back.
Good-bye, good-bye, my smarties,
Time to go. . . . Line up, please!

You can play line-up games, too. You ran out of time today. You didn't have time to review. So play a learning game. Have the kids line up by height, or by the color of their shoes or shirts. Or pick a color and say that anyone wearing that color gets to be toward the front of the line. You say, "Anyone who has red on and gets over here gets to be first." And they're looking at one another and saying, "You have red on!" You're getting them to play games at the same time you're trying to get them to do something organizational.

You can use a poem or make up a song. The rule is that by the time I get to the end of the song, you need to be in line.

Another Good Closing Song

When the Day Is Done
(*To the tune of "Where Is Thumbkin?"*)
Off to your house, off to your house,
Our day's done, our day's done.
We'll be back together, we'll be back together.
Tomorrow, tomorrow.

Saying Good-bye

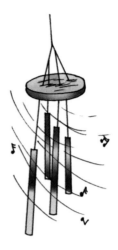

When the kids are lining up at the end of Afternoon Wrap-Up, have them line up in the order of their birthdays, names, or shoe sizes. (They may not know their shoe sizes, but they definitely know how to stand there and compare how big their feet are!) Maybe everybody who's wearing something blue gets to be at the head of the line. If they're going to line up in a single row, then they need to turn and say good-bye. They can shake hands, or they can wave. Sometimes I ask each child to shake the hand of the person behind him and the person in front of him. If they don't want to shake hands, they can give a hug, a high five, or a hand wave.

I do ask them to use one another's names. I like it when they get to the point where they say the name and then say, "See you later, alligator." They joke about it: "See you in the morning. Don't be snoring." One of the kids started saying, "See you in the morning, and tonight don't be snoring," and he thought it was funnier than heck.

HOW I BELIEVE CHILDREN LEARN BEST

The way in which we choose to begin and end our days in classrooms across the United States speaks volumes about what we value. We value kids' learning through reading, writing, listening, speaking, and viewing. We want to set the stage for the next day, and we want to emphasize the shared responsibility in the class. I'm not the only teacher. I'm not the one with all the information. We can share what we've learned and play off that. I want to build problem-solvers. I want to teach kids to solve their own problems because when I do, I'll buy myself more time for teaching. When we're not the answer to all their problems, that's the day when we'll have more time for teaching in our classrooms.

I want to highlight my belief in how children learn best: they learn by doing, and they learn by sharing what they've learned with someone else. How often do you let a child be the teacher? We know a child has mastered something if she can teach it to someone else. I want to offer safety, to build classrooms where kids know how to speak to one another and feel safe doing so. I don't want them to feel, "Well, what if I have the wrong answer? I can't speak up." That's one reason we're always sharing, to help them feel safe.

I want to develop a climate of trust, in which we learn to depend on one another. I want my kids to know that what they said is something I might use at home tonight with *my* mother. And what they just did? Tomorrow I'm going to try that. And I want to cement the community, because with a community, kids are going to be at their optimal learning level.

WHAT'S YOUR PHILOSOPHY?

Make sure you know your own philosophy of how kids learn best. What's best for them? Live by that philosophy. Know why you did what you did today. And make sure that when you're looking forward and closing the day, you think about how those kids learn best and what you did today that played into that philosophy. "I had fun" isn't good enough anymore. We're in a country of high-stakes standards. "I had fun"? No. "I had fun, and I went back to those essential questions that I was trying to teach today and that we talked about in Morning Meeting."

Help the Substitute Stick to Your Routine

You don't want a sub to change the classroom routine—but to stick to the routine, she has to know what it is.
The best way to keep to your Morning Meeting, Afternoon Wrap-Up routine when you're out is to keep a book that's ready to go. It's great if you can set it up so that the kids can just walk through the pages and the book actually shows the routine to the sub. Open the book and the first page says, "Each morning we gather at ____ [fill in the time]." The next line says, "We do this to greet each other." And you fill it in. Maybe it just lists the four Hs. And the kids know what that means. The sub doesn't, but she can follow the book, and the kids can explain anything she doesn't know.

Maybe the next thing the book says is "We do an interactive chart. The kids can help you.

Morning Message needs to begin this way; then please just improvise and add whatever you'd like." It's in book form, and it walks them through the routine. That way the kids can't say, "Well, we don't do that!"

Create a page for each step. The substitute doesn't have to use all the pages, just the ones she wants. You might name the games you play in class. Maybe you know you've really worked on Mum Ball. So in the back of the book, where you talk about Afternoon Wrap-Up, you might say, "Please play Mum Ball based on these things."

I'll end this book in the same way I often end my presentations: by sharing with you one of my favorite quotes, from Danny Cox: "The important thing to remember is that if you don't have that inspired enthusiasm that's contagious, whatever you do have is also contagious."

You can make Morning Meeting and Afternoon Wrap-Up as exciting and as fun and as big a learning experience as you want them to be.

RESOURCES

BIBLIOGRAPHY

Bloom, B. S. (ed.). *Taxonomy of Educational Objectives: The Classification of Educational Goals. Handbook I: Cognitive Domain.* New York, Toronto: Longmans, Green, 1956.

Charles, C. *Building Classroom Discipline* (7th ed.). Classroom management programs stress the importance of community building in successful management. Boston: Allyn & Bacon, 2002.

Charney, R. S. *Teaching Children to Care: Management in the Responsive Classroom.* Greenfield, Mass.: Northeast Foundation for Children, 1992.

Emmer, E. T. *Classroom Management: Research and Implications* (R & D Report No. 6178). Austin, Tex.: Research and Development Center for Teacher Education, University of Texas (ERIC Document Reproduction Service No. ED251448), 1984.

Emmer, E. T., Sanford, J. P., Evertson, C. M., Clements, B. S., and Martin, J. *The Classroom Management Improvement Study: An Experiment in Elementary School Classrooms* (R & D Report No. 6050). Austin, Tex.: Research and Development Center for Teacher Education, University of Texas (ERIC Document Reproduction Service No. ED226452), 1981.

Glasser, W. *Choice Theory: A New Psychology of Personal Freedom.* New York: HarperCollins, 1998.

Glasser, W. "A New Look at School Failure and School Success." *Phi Delta Kappan* v78 n8 p596–602, April 1997.

Wong, H. and Wong, R. *The First Days of School: How to Be an Effective Teacher.* Mountain View, Calif.: Harry K. Wong Publications, Inc., 1998.

INDEX

A

ABCs of My Day
   chart, *102*
   letter about, *100*
   losing, 106
   purpose of, 98–99, 101, 103, 105–7
Afternoon Wrap-Up
   components of, 92
      ABCs of My Day, 98–99, *100,* 101, *102,* 103, 105–7
      checklists and reminder notes, 110–13, *114–16*
      closing activities, 95, 149–51
      games for review and assessment, 123–48
      pack-up time, 95, 97
      preparation for the Desk Fairy, 119–20, *121*
      Report Card for the Teacher, 107–8, *109*
      sharing, 117
      song, 122
      story reading, 118
   flexibility with, 96
   purposes of, 91–92, 94–95
Alphabet, teaching, in Morning Message, 48
Anger, how to express, 104, 110
Announcements, during Morning Meeting, 64
Arrivals, activities during, 37–38
Assessment time, 16–17
Associative memory, vs. rote memory, 93
Attendance-Go-Round, for Morning Greeting, 39
Attention spans of children, 65
Attitude, in ABCs of My Day, 99, *100, 102,* 103, 105, 106

B

Beanie Baby, for Mum Ball, 124, 125
Beat the Clock game, 148
Before and after, calendar for teaching, 76
Behavior
   in ABCs of My Day, 98, 99, *100,* 101, *102,* 103, 105
   changing, 106, 110
   modeling, 104, 106–7, 139
Belonging, as psychological need, 15
Benefits of Morning Meeting and Afternoon Wrap-Up, 16
Bloom, B.S., 14
Bloom's Taxonomy, 14
Book Treasures, 118–19
Bucket of the Five Senses game, 142, *143*

C

Calendar activities, for teaching
   before and after, 76
   date, 73
   geometry, 76, 77
   graphing, 77
   holidays, 77
   mathematical language, 77
   money concepts, 74
   morning and nighttime, 76
   number sense, 76
   odd and even, 74, *75*
   patterning, 76
   place value, 77
   seasons, 77, *78*
   sequencing, 77
   skip counting, 76, 77
   time of day, 76
   yesterday, today, and tomorrow, 76
Cellophane, for calendar highlighting, 77
Chair
   signs for, 28, *31*
   uses for, 28
Chaos in mornings and afternoons, 11–12
Charades, 131
Charles, C., 13
Checklists
   everyday, 110–11, *114*
   "I Need," 112, *114*
Choices, good vs. bad, 104
Choice theory, 14–15, 25
Circle seating, for meetings, 29, 30
Classes, naming, 42
Clocks, for schedule, 67, *69*
Closing, in Afternoon Wrap-Up, 95, 149–51
Color coding
   in ABCs of My Day, 99, 101, 103, 105–6
   in Morning Message, 43
Community building
   as basic need, 23
   from classroom management, 13
   evaluated in ABCs of My Day, 99, *100, 102,* 105, 106
   for learning success, 152
   from Morning Meeting and Afternoon Wrap-Up, 18
Computer News, for interactive bulletin board, 84
Controlling students
   teachers' methods of, 20, 22
   by teaching self-control, 25
Cookie patterns, for teaching odd and even, 74, *75*
Country theme, for interactive bulletin board, 85
Crowns, in Guess Crowns game, 140–41

Note: Page numbers in italics indicate reproducibles.

D

"DA," in ABCs of My Day, 103
Date
    calendar for teaching, 73
    in Morning Message, 45–46
Desk Fairy, 119–20, *121*
Difficult students, dealing with, 19–20, 22
Directionality, teaching, in Morning Message, 46, 47, 49

E

Editing skills, learned from Morning Message, 63
Eggs-traordinary Kids, for interactive bulletin board, 81, *82*
Essential questions
    determining students' understanding of, 96–97
    returning to, in Afternoon Wrap-Up, 94–95, 153
Evaluation of day, in Afternoon Wrap-Up, 92, 95
Everyday checklists, 110–11, *114*

F

Face, revealing child's mood, 34
Forgotten items
    home/school folders, 37, 98
    preventing, with checklists and reminders, 110–13, *114–16*
Four Hs, for Morning Greeting, 38–39
Freedom, as psychological need, 15
Fun, as psychological need, 15
Fun bags, 111
Future bottle, for Predicting the Future game, 145

G

Games for review and assessment
    Beat the Clock, 148
    Bucket of the Five Senses, 142, *143*
    Charades, 131
    Guess Crowns, 140–41
    Hey, What Do You Say?, 134
    I Have/Who Has?, 146, *147*
    Mum Ball, 124–25
    plan book as reminder in, 145
    Predicting the Future, 144–45
    Secret Ballot, 128–29, *130*
    That's Bogus, 132
    Venn Diagram, 135
    What Adam Missed, 136–37, *138*
    What If Mom or Dad Asks?, 133
    What? Where? How? When? Who? Why?, 146
    Who Wants to Be a Smartie?, 126–27
    Who Wants to Be the Teacher?, 139
Geometry, calendar for teaching, 76, 77
Give Me Words, for interactive bulletin board, 84, *138*

G

Glasser, William, 14, 25
Goals for Morning Meeting and Afternoon Wrap-Up
    building community, 13
    developing higher-level thinking skills, 14
    establishing routine, 13–14
    helping kids succeed, 14–15
    integrating components of teaching literacy, 14
    providing time for assessment and reflection, 16–17
Good-byes, at close of day, 151
Graphic organizers, 137
    hamburger, 84, *87*
    quote bubbles, 136–37, *138*
    Venn diagrams, 135
Graphing, calendar for teaching, 77
Guess Crowns game, 140–41

H

Hamburger, for interactive bulletin board, 84, *87*
Hey, What Do You Say? game, 134
Higher-level thinking skills, developing, 14, 140–41
Highlighting, in ABCs of My Day, 98, 99, 101, 103
Holidays, calendar for teaching, 77
Home/school folders
    checklists in, 110–11, 112
    forgotten, 37, 98
    labels for, 99
    letter about, *35*
    packing up, 97, 98
    purpose of, 34, 36–37
Homework, 111

I

I Have/Who Has? game, 146, *147*
"I Need" checklist, 112, *114*
"I Need to Remember" note, 112, *115*
    teaching opportunity from, 113
Interactive bulletin board
    purpose of, 79
    themes for
        Computer News, 84
        Country, 85
        Eggs-traordinary Kids, 81, *82*
        Give Me Words, 84, *138*
        Hamburger, 84, *87*
        Keys to Speaking (or Keys to Writing or Keys to Reading), 84, *89*
        no-think chart, 85, 86, *90*
        Planet, 85
        Smartie Publishing's Newest Titles, 83
        Smartieville, 80
        Tool Board, 83, *88*
        Welcome to Our Neighborhood, 79–80

Note: Page numbers in italics indicate reproducibles.

We're a Perfect Fit, 83
What Lives Here?, 84
What Would You Ask?, 80–81
Who Would You Like to See "Pop" In?, 83
Interactive chart
    for Morning Message (*see* Morning Message)
    for teaching standards, 48
Interests, determining, in Afternoon Wrap-Up, 94

J
Jobs, classroom, assigning student teachers for, 26–27

K
Keys to Speaking (or Keys to Writing or Keys to Reading), for interactive bulletin board, 84, *89*
Kind words, modeling, 104

L
Labels for home/school folders, 99
Language, kind vs. angry, 104
Learning
    best means of, 152
    five components of, 14, 40
    meeting basic needs for, 24
    philosophy about, 153–54
    unmet needs affecting, 23
Lesson evaluation, in Afternoon Wrap-Up, 94
Lesson plans, alternatives to, 50
Letter cases, teaching, in Morning Message, 48
Letters
    about ABCs of My Day, *100*
    from Desk Fairy, *121*
    about home/school folder, *35*
Line-up games, at close of day, 150–51
Looking forward, in Afternoon Wrap-Up, 95
Lucky Ducks, for taking turns, 141

M
Mailboxes, 97
Managing students, 113
Maslow, Abraham, 13
Maslow's Hierarchy of Needs, *22–24*
Math concepts, calendar for teaching, 73–77
Mathematical language, calendar for teaching, 77
Meeting area
    arranging, 28–30, 32
    rules for, 29
"Me" folders, 62
Mistakes, in Morning Message, 56
Modeling behavior, 104, 106–7, 139
Money concepts, calendar for teaching, 74
Mood of child, face revealing, 34
Morning and nighttime, calendar for teaching, 76

Morning Greeting, 33, 38–39
Morning Meeting
    components of
        activities during arrivals, 37–38
        assessing child's mood, 34
        calendar, 73–78
        home/school folder, 34–37
        interactive bulletin boards, 79–86
        Morning Greeting, 33, 38–39
        Morning Message (*see* Morning Message)
        movement through song, 65–66
        schedule, 67–72
        starting signal, 38
    outline for, 47
Morning Message
    addressing standards in, 46–49
    for building sight word vocabulary, 51, *52*
    color coding, 43
    date on, 45–46
    including everyone in, 57–61, 63
    including students' names in, 62
    including student teacher in, 62–63
    mistakes in, 56
    picture clues in, 53, *54, 55, 71, 72*
    pointers for, 61
    purpose of, 40–41
    for reinforcement, 49–51
    repetition in, 41–42, 46
    rereading, for connecting writing and reading, 63
    sample, from later in the year, 60
    school announcements during, 64
    student involvement in, 37–38, 45, 49
    summary of hints for, 63
    time needed for, 61
Movement, in Morning Meeting, 65–66
Mum Ball game, 124–25

N
Names for classes, 42
Nonverbal signals, during meetings, 21, *44*
No-think chart, for interactive bulletin board, 85, 86, *90*
Number sense, calendar for teaching, 76

O
Odd and even, calendar for teaching, 74, *75*
"Oops" slips, 112–13, *116*
Overview/review, in Afternoon Wrap-Up, 94, 96–97

P
Pack-up time, in Afternoon Wrap-Up, 95, 97
Patterning, calendar for teaching, 76
Philosophy about learning, 153–54

Note: Page numbers in italics indicate reproducibles.

Physiological needs, in Maslow's Hierarchy of Needs, 22–23

Picture clues
for calendar, 77, *78*
in Morning Message, 53, *54, 55, 71, 72*
in schedule, 70, *71, 72*

Place value, calendar for teaching, 77

Plan book, as reminder in game playing, 145

Planet theme, for interactive bulletin board, 85

Pocket chart, for schedule, 67–68

Poems, for movement in Morning Meeting, 65, 66

Pointers, for Morning Message, 61

"Popcorn" song, 66

Popcorn words, for exposing sight words, 51, *52*

Power
children's need for, 25
as psychological need, 15
restoring, for children, 104

Predicting the Future game, 144–45

Problem solving, helping students develop skills for, 24–25, 106–7, 152

Promises, avoiding, in schedule, 70

Psychological needs, as key to successful learning, 14–15

Punctuation, teaching, in Morning Message, 47, 48

Q

Questioning students
for opening up lessons, 57–61
about their school day, 92, 93

Question practice, for interactive bulletin board, 80–81

Quote bubbles, 84, 136–37, *138*

R

Reading
in Afternoon Wrap-Up, 118–19, 134
importance of, 118

Red pen, in ABCs of My Day, 105, 106

Reminders
checklists, 110–12, *114*
"I Need to Remember" note, 112, *115*
"Oops" slips, 112–13, *116*

Report Card for the Teacher, 107–8, *109*

Reproducibles
ABCs of My Day chart, *102*
ABCs of My Day letter, *100*
for Bucket of the Five Senses game, *143*
chair-sharing signs, *31*
cookie patterns, *75*
Desk Fairy letter, *121*
Eggs-traordinary Kids, *82*
everyday checklists, *114*
hamburger, *87*

home/school folder letter, *35*
for I Have/Who Has? game, *147*
"I Need" checklists, *114*
"I Need to Remember" notes, *115*
keys, *89*
nonverbal signals, *44*
no-think chart, *90*
"Oops" slips, *116*
picture clues, *54, 55, 71, 72*
popcorn words, *52*
quote bubbles, *138*
Report Card for the Teacher, *109*
schedule clocks, *69*
season clue cards, *78*
Secret Ballot, *130*
for time stick, *44*
tool board, *88*

Resources, 155

Review and assessment games. *See* Games for review and assessment

Rhymes
for Morning Greeting, 39
for seeing students to the door, 149

Routines, established from Morning Meeting and Afternoon Wrap-Up, 13–14

Row rotation, for meetings, 29–30

Rules
importance of setting, 25
sample, 29

S

Safety needs
in Maslow's Hierarchy of Needs, 23
unmet, interfering with learning, 23

Schedule
announcing changes in, 67
avoiding promises about, 70
clocks for, 67, *69*
making, 67–68
picture clues in, 70, *71, 72*
warning signals about, 70

School announcements, during Morning Meeting, 64

School supplies, "I Need" checklist for, 112

Seasons, calendar for teaching, 77, *78*

Secret Ballot game, 128–29, *130*

Self-actualization, in Maslow's Hierarchy of Needs, 24

Self-control, teaching students to have, 25

Sequencing, calendar for teaching, 77

Sharing, in Afternoon Wrap-Up, 117

Sight words
building exposure to, 51
popcorn words highlighting, 51, *52*
reinforcing, 50–51

Note: Page numbers in italics indicate reproducibles.

Signal, starting Morning Meeting, 38
Signs, for chair sharing, 28, *31*
Sing Yourself Smart CD, 150
Skip counting, calendar for teaching, 76, 77
Smartie Publishing's Newest Titles, for interactive bulletin board, 83
Smartieville bulletin board, for reviewing concepts, 80
Smiley and grouchy faces as nonverbal signals, 21, *44*
Social skills, learned from Morning Greeting, 39
Songs
    in Afternoon Wrap-Up, 122
    for line-up, 150
    for Morning Greeting, 39
    for movement in Morning Meeting, 65–66
Sounds, teaching, in Morning Message, 48
Spacing, teaching, in Morning Message, 46–47
Speech bubbles. *See* Quote bubbles
Standards
    addressing, in Morning Message, 46–49
    meeting, 18
    opportunities for teaching, 50
Story reading, in Afternoon Wrap-Up, 118–19, 134
Student teacher
    in Afternoon Wrap-Up, 98
    assigning students as, 26–27
    in Morning Message, 62–63
    requesting help, 101
Substitutes, classroom routine book for, 153
Success in school, meeting psychological needs for, 14–15
Syllables, teaching, in Morning Message, 48

T
Talk Back, during Mum Ball, 124–25
That's Bogus game, 132
Think time, time stick for, 43, *44*
Thumbs-up and thumbs-down nonverbal signals, 21, *44*
Time management, 68
Time of day, teaching, 67, 68, 70, 76
Time saving, from Morning Meeting and Afternoon Wrap-Up, 17
Time stick, 43, *44*
Tool Board, for interactive bulletin board, 83, *88*
Tools for Morning Meeting and Afternoon Wrap-Up, 41
T-shirt cutout, for interactive bulletin board, 79–80
Turn taking, Lucky Ducks for, 141

V
Venn diagrams, 135

W
Welcome to Our Neighborhood, for interactive bulletin board, 79–80
We're a Perfect Fit, for interactive bulletin board, 83
What Adam Missed game, 136–37, *138*
What If Mom or Dad Asks? game, 133
What Lives Here?, for interactive bulletin board, 84
What? Where? How? When? Who? Why? game, 146
What Would You Ask?, for interactive bulletin board, 80–81
Whining, 106–7
Who Wants to Be a Smartie? game, 126–27
Who Wants to Be the Teacher? game, 139
Who Would You Like to See "Pop" In?, for interactive bulletin board, 83

Y
Yesterday, today, and tomorrow, calendar for teaching, 76
You Read to Me, I'll Read to You (Hoberman), 43

Z
Ziploc bags, in home/school folders, 36

Note: Page numbers in italics indicate reproducibles.